"This book is a must read for balls in the air, all the plates s fire—more than just another self-help, 'If I could only get more organized approach to managing our lives and the lives of our loved ones. The wisdom born in Susie's own life, delivered with her 'let's get real' enthusiasm, is the secret key you always knew existed and have been searching for. It's time to surrender our own expectations. Now that is what I call a liberated woman."

—LISA RYAN, author; speaker; TV personality:
*InTouch with Charles Stanley, 700 Club*

"If you are feeling overwhelmed and overloaded, then this book is for you! Susie Davis will give you permission to slow down and will inspire you to find the deeper rest that you long for."

—DR. SAM ADAMS, coauthor, *Out of Control: Finding Peace for the Physically Exhausted* and *Spiritually Strung Out*

"Susie Davis offers the most help with nagging time issues I've ever received—by asking us to look not at the hours and minutes, but at ourselves. This book can be a life-changer."

—NANCY RUE, author of the best-selling Lily and Sophie series

"I count it an honor to endorse Susie Davis's debut book, *The Time of Your Life*. Susie tackles a topic that plagues a majority of Christian women, myself included. Her transparent and authentic writing style makes the book a pleasure to read from start to finish. Reading this book is time well spent and a wise investment in your future!"

—VICKI COURTNEY, founder of Virtuous Reality Ministries, national speaker, and best-selling author of *Your Girl* and *TeenVirtue*

"This book is a timely reminder of the dangers that flow from a breathless lifestyle. Susie candidly presents insights for those who struggle with illusive time management."

—JACKIE KENDALL, best-selling author of *Lady in Waiting*

# The Time of Your Life

SUSIE DAVIS

# The Time of YOUR Life

## Finding God's Rest in Your Busy Schedule

CROSSWAY BOOKS

A PUBLISHING MINISTRY OF
GOOD NEWS PUBLISHERS
WHEATON, ILLINOIS

Cover design: Josh Dennis

Cover photo: Getty Images

First printing, 2006

Printed in the United States of America

**Library of Congress Cataloging-in-Publication Data**
Davis, Susie, 1963–
   The time of your life : finding God's rest in your busy schedule /
Susie Davis.
    p. cm.
   ISBN 13: 978-1-58134-752-4
   ISBN 10: 1-58134-752-9 (tpb)
   1. Employees—Religious life. 2. Work—Religious aspects—
Christianity. I. Title.
BV4593.D38    2005
248.4—dc22                       2005032175

| BP | | 16 | 15 | 14 | 13 | 12 | 11 | 10 | 09 | 08 | 07 | 06 |
|----|----|----|----|----|----|----|----|----|----|----|----|----|
| 15 | 14 | 13 | 12 | 11 | 10 | 9 | 8 | 7 | 6 | 5 | 4 | 3 | 2 | 1 |

To
JESUS CHRIST:

*Whom have I in heaven but you?*
*And there is nothing on earth that I desire besides you.*
PSALM 73:25

# Contents

# Acknowledgments

**To my husband, Will,** and our children Will III, Emily, and Sara: Thank you for making life unspeakably beautiful. And thank you for being so patient with me as I spent time writing this book.

To my parents, Bob and Peg Gerrie, for their relentless encouragement of ministry fulfillment in my life.

To Vicki Courtney: For clearing the path ahead of me with such wisdom.

To Bill Jensen: Thank you for believing in me and in this project—and for endless questions answered.

And to Anne Christian Buchanan: For your creative and thoughtful editing of this work.

# Introduction

**Could you use a little rest?** A little balance? A little more time to do what you need to do—or even better, what you *want* to do?

Even without knowing you, I believe your answer is yes. I believe that because almost every woman I know feels that way at least some of the time.

Think honestly—when was the last time you had a break, or at least a break unaccompanied by feelings of guilt or panic or some other clock-induced discomfort? When was the last time you felt fully rested, fully relaxed, fully in tune with what God wants for your life?

We live in a clock-watching culture. We're surrounded by the blinking and ticking and buzzing of clocks and watches, all of them pestering us to move along. They trail our schedules, hounding us until we finally collapse in bed at night, then blast us bleary-eyed into morning.

In the last fifty years, especially, the explosion of technology has pulled us into a rhythm that would have seemed quite unnatural for our ancestors. If you're like me, you're moving as fast as you can, breathing little prayers to God for help as you careen from item to item on your packed to-do list.

Sometimes you're wired, sailing along on a caffeine and adrenaline high, feeling the rush and the satisfaction of getting things done, but secretly wondering how long you can keep it up.

Sometimes you're tired, putting one foot in front of another and trudging through your schedule, but never daring to stop for fear you'd never get going again.

And sometimes you're just doing what needs to be done, aware that there has to be more to life than what you're living—but who has time to stop and figure it out?

Do you ever feel a tug at your soul to slow down and spend time with God, but you have this overwhelming sense that if you do that, you'll just get further behind? I know I do. All too often as much as I desire a sane and balanced life, the pull of my schedule seems to shoot me into overdrive. And I'm not a Wall Street executive. The fate of nations doesn't hang on my getting things done. I am what you are—an ordinary woman living an ordinary life that sometimes feels out of control. I am a pastor's wife and the mother of three. I work part-time in a ministry position, supervise a household, run the typical mothering taxi service, ride horses for fun and exercise, squeeze in my writing wherever I can—and try my best to keep it all together.

Do I always succeed? Unfortunately no. But I'm getting much better. Step by stumbling step, I've been learning to back off and accept the rest that is available for each of us, even in the midst of our hectic schedules. I'm learning that God really does have a plan for those of us who struggle with a lack of time in a busy schedule. And what He offers is not another endless list of to-dos, not even a new scheme for managing time. Instead, the One who created time in the first place offers us a whole new vision for the days and minutes of our lives. A new vision of what life can mean—purposeful, exciting, and yet filled with His peace.

The purpose of *The Time of Your Life* is to share with you some of what I've been learning about God and His design for our schedules and our lives. A lot of it concerns time, yet this is not really a time-management book. And although I'll suggest some practical steps for changing the way you handle your time (and some down-to-earth Time Out exercises at the end of every chapter), this is not fundamentally a self-help, "get organized" book.

If you're like me, you already have a couple of those (or a dozen) on your bookshelves. And books like that have a lot to offer. But few of them ever get to the root of our problems with time and schedule—which involves facing who we are, who God made us to be, and all the ways our fallen nature and our warp-speed culture can pull us away from what God has in mind. It's my firm belief that until we get those matters straight, no amount of organization in the world will give us what we really need.

My prayer for you upon reading this book is not that you will become queen of the organizational charts. Instead, I pray you will fall more deeply in love with God and will understand His will for you in a more whole fashion. I pray you will move from yearning for more time to actually claiming your schedule and getting real joy out of your time here on earth.

That kind of joy translates into loving God and His people in an authentic and timely way. It's the kind of joy that can nudge you to a new level of spirituality, a rediscovery of God and His plan for you and a new understanding of what it really means to rest in God.

*Rest.* It's a beautiful word, isn't it? You and I could both use a little more of it. But have you ever considered that rest is not only a privilege but a God-given *right*? Not only that, it's a divine *commandment*—the Lord has actually given us orders to slow down and rest. I've come to believe that rest is actually the key to a purposeful life. When you build a life in which rest balances activity, you can actually outpace those who are always driven and in a hurry.

God has promises for those of us who choose to live by His guidelines. Don't miss out on the success of living life at a God-designed pace. You'll love your life if you follow His principles. No more exhausted, fruitless living. No more always being tired and busy.

Understanding God's view of time can catapult joy directly into your life as you uncover His truth about time.

Your time.

His time.

Truly, the time of your life!

PART ONE

# All in the Time in the World:

Rethinking Your Hectic Life . . .
from God's Point of View

# The Time of Your Life

*"I have all the time in the world."*

*Don't you wish you could speak that phrase honestly? The words have such a luxurious feel. They suggest an abundance of a resource that often feels painfully scarce.*

*The truth is, we could never speak those words honestly because time isn't ours in the first place. Though we spend time, we don't really own it. And though time shapes our lives and choices, it's never really under our control.*

*Only one Being holds and controls all the time in the world—God. As the Creator of time and space, He holds the ultimate knowledge of what time is and how it is best spent. So the only truly effective way for us to enjoy the riches of God's time is to draw closer to Him and glean our understanding about time from Him. This section provides a beginning point for doing just that.*

*As you read these chapters, remember that God holds the keys to your time struggles, your scheduling woes, your worry and exhaustion.*

*He wants you to share in His abundance, to show you how to live more purposefully and joyfully.*

*Best of all, He's there for you always.*

*After all, He does have all the time in the world!*

# 1

# A Fresh Perspective:

## Why It's Not Really "My Time"

**I have had a few epiphanies** in my life that defy description. One such event involved climbing the mountains in Estes Park, Colorado. A friend and I had decided on a lake hike, an uncomplicated six-mile round-trip. We had just emerged from an area of dense forest and turned to climb slightly higher before we spiraled down toward a nestled lake. When I crested the rise and looked down toward the lake, I was surprised by a breathtaking sight—a gigantic mountain reflected on the surface of the water. And then the epiphany. I lifted my eyes to see what was reflected—the monumental mountain itself.

It was a moment filled with awe. I wept, silenced and stunned by the grandness of God's handiwork, weakened by the beauty of it, and overwhelmed by His love for me—a very small me. A speck in a grand world of tremendous landscapes. A tiny speck of humanity in a world full of millions of people. A speck of life history in hundreds of thousands of years of lifetimes.

I realized then, as if for the first time, that God is *very big* and I am *very small*. It was a life-changing experience for me, one that brought an inexplicable truth to my life.

A change of perspective can do that for a person. Shifting the way we look at things can make all the difference in the way we live our lives—and the way we handle our time. Understanding time from God's perspective and adapting ourselves to His view can truly revolutionize the way we handle our schedules.

So what is God's perspective on time? The very first pages of the Bible make it clear:

> *In the beginning, God created the heavens and the earth. The earth was without form and void, and darkness was over the face of the deep. And the Spirit of God was hovering over the face of the waters. And God said, "Let there be light," and there was light. And God saw that the light was good. And God separated the light from the darkness. God called the light Day, and the darkness he called Night. And there was evening and there was morning, the first day. (Genesis 1:1-5)*

Time, in other words, was one of God's earliest acts of creation. First He formed the heavens and the earth. Matter. Bulk. We can see it and touch it. But His very next act was to separate light from darkness, and that was the beginning of time as we know it.

Time—invisible and untouchable, yet ticking away. A piece of God's original, intangible artwork, mysterious and elusive, framed only by day and night. From the beginning we've tried to grab it, hold it, and manage it. It remains a steady work, set in motion by God, and we are still unable to get our hands around it.

As awed as I am at the mountains in Colorado and the ocean's expansive hold on the Texas border, I am absolutely flabbergasted at God's design of time. It sits bookended by eternity itself, its start and finish beyond human description. Try as we may to see it and conquer it, it moves on, unstoppable.

And yet God maintains an absolute hold over time. He is its Creator, its resolute Master. If we were able to see all of time as we know it, from the earliest record of man to this moment's headline news, and then were able to frame this monstrous time line, in all its enormity . . . it still would dangle beneath God's little finger. This massive, unprecedented, impregnable masterpiece is dwarfed by the greatness of the One who made it.

## A Fresh Perspective:
## Why It's Not Really "My Time"

**Time is perpetual innovation, a synonym for continuous creation. Time is God's gift to the world of space. A world in time is a world going on through God; realization of an infinite design; not a thing in itself but a thing for God. (Joshua Heschel)**

That is the way God sees time. He views all time—our personal days and hours and the history of time itself—as a tiny part of His very large plan. It exists because He dreamed it up. He maintains it with no effort or worry. He knows its beginning from its end, its possibilities and its limitations. Time remains under His complete authority, His undisturbed control. And it is one of God's greatest gifts to us—a workable framework in which we can live our lives and accomplish His will and develop a relationship with Him.

And yet how many of us think of time that way? I know I don't always (though I try). Instead, I struggle against time. I struggle within it. I waste time. I try to hold it too tightly. And all too often I see it as a nemesis instead of a gift.

I think, *I'd really like to get involved with that ministry . . . or read that book . . . or exercise more . . . but I don't have time.*

Or I look back at what I had hoped to accomplish in life and grow depressed because the years are ticking away faster than I had planned.

Or I get held up in a meeting or a conversation or a traffic jam and fuss and fume because other people are "wasting my time."

But that's just the problem, I think, or a big part of it. I get obsessed with "my time" because I lose perspective. I lose track of the basic truth that time *isn't* mine.

Surely our greatest frustrations with time all begin with that faulty assumption that our time belongs to us—that we're in charge of how our lives unfold, that we can control our minutes and hours. The truth is, we'll never come to terms with time until we understand God's view on time.

Simply put, all time belongs to Him. He lends each of us an allotted amount of time for our use, but our time is ours only to use, not to own. And we're responsible to the Creator of time for how we treat His gift.

In the Gospel of Mark we find a fascinating exchange between Jesus and the Pharisees. It's not specifically about time, but it does illuminate this basic idea of ownership. It started when the Pharisees asked Jesus a question:

> "Teacher, we know that you are true and do not care about anyone's opinion. For you are not swayed by appearances, but truly teach the way of God. Is it lawful to pay taxes to Caesar, or not? Should we pay them, or should we not?" But, knowing their hypocrisy, he said to them, "Why put me to the test? Bring me a denarius and let me look at it." And they brought one. And he said to them, "Whose likeness and inscription is this?" They said to him, "Caesar's." Jesus said to them, "Render to Caesar the things that are Caesar's, and to God the things that are God's." And they marveled at him. (12:14-17)

Now the Pharisees asked their question to trap Jesus, but they ended up entrapping themselves. And I wonder if we sometimes do the same thing when it comes to time.

Jesus asked the Pharisees to look at the face on the denarius, a Roman coin. Clearly it was Caesar's likeness and belonged to Caesar. But do we have a scope of imagination large enough to look on time and recognize whose likeness it bears—who owns it, who's in charge?

God's image is unmistakably stamped on the face of all time. But the problem is, we rarely think that way—at least not when it comes to that minuscule slice of time that makes up our own lives.

I know that's true of me. When I talk about "my time," I tend to stuff my perception of time into a small frame, a cheap reproduction. I forget that God is giving me minutes and hours and days and is allowing me the freedom to choose how to use them. Time is one of His greatest gifts—granting us stewardship, letting us loose with His precious time. God lets us handle His masterpiece day by day, knowing full well it may be squandered or underappreciated. Most artists couldn't bear to see their creation so undervalued.

So here's a question to consider: when you look at your watch, do you think of the minutes as being your own? Do you look down at it, silently cursing at whatever takes away minutes and hours and days you wanted to spend your way? Do you ever remember to think about your time as God's time and wonder how He wants you to use it? Have you ever searched for the face of your watch, seeing those hands tick away, and considered that those minutes are a reflection of the artistry of God?

I must say that such occasions in my own life have been rare. Yet when I have managed to keep that basic reality in mind, when I have tried to see my time from God's perspective and to render to God what is God's, my schedule frustrations have almost always been eased.

Jesus was always exhorting His disciples to get some eyes that could see. He meant learning to look at things in a spiritual sense, to see things God's way. He explained that seeing with spiritual eyes, through God's perspective, was a key to happiness and joy in life. "But blessed are your eyes, for they see," He said, "and your ears, for they hear" (Matthew 13:16).

I need some more of that, and I suspect you do too. I want the blessing that comes with seeing all of life—including time—from God's frame of reference. And seeing things God's way has to begin with realizing how often we *don't* see that way. Only when we realize how limited our perception is can we start viewing things afresh.

We clearly have two options: the worldly view and the spiritual view. The worldly outlook says, "This time is mine. I possess it. And I need lots more of it."

The spiritual view counters, "This time is a gift. God has entrusted me with it. *God, please help me discover the best way to use it.*"

**Time is but the stream I go a-fishing in. I drink at it; but while I drink I see the sandy bottom and detect how shallow it is. Its thin current slides away, but eternity remains. I would drink deeper; fish in the sky, whose bottom is pebbly with stars. (Henry David Thoreau)**

How do we achieve such a spiritually based outlook? To a large degree, it involves changing our habits of thinking. We must be willing consciously to relinquish our perceptions of control and yield to

God's eternal perspective. And we need to do that again and again, exposing ourselves to the truth through prayer and Bible study and fellowship with other believers, reminding ourselves again and again of the truth about time until our thought habits begin to change.

In my own life I have found that the most significant change in my thinking has come about by my strategically inputting God's Word in my mind and in my heart. I tend to think of myself as fragile without a constant drip of the Bible into my daily life. So my morning starts with reading the Word and praying. That is followed by listening to a Bible teacher on TV or radio. I often listen to Christian music while driving the kids to school or running errands. And I try to remind myself every time I am outside to look up—literally—and remember who is in charge.

One small area of my life where my new habits have paid off is driving in traffic. I tend to think I can get to a certain location in a set amount of time. And while that may sometimes be true, it does not always happen in Austin, Texas, where I live. It's a growing city with lots of construction and unpredictable, frustrating traffic jams, and these have been a frequent source of irritation to me. I've been known to rant and rave, feeling as though the traffic tangles were stealing my time. Then I realized that, honestly, I cannot control the traffic anymore than I control the clock. And after accepting the truth of that, I was able to relax a little, knowing that God is aware of what's going on with the traffic. He's just as sovereign over the time it takes to move me from here to there as He is over the rest of time.

Does that revised perspective mean I never get frustrated in traffic these days? No, but it really has helped. Remembering that God is in control helps keep my stress levels lower. I've learned to accept traffic as a reality and to be more diligent about seeking God's wisdom about my scheduling choices. I've even started wondering what I had hoped to do with that few minutes I thought I "lost" in traffic.

God's desire for us to have an eternal perspective in life most certainly includes our time. And though our limited human brains could never take in the whole scope of His work, that does not excuse us from exerting ourselves to His best purpose. We need to be a people set on the tremendous task of ever yielding to God's teaching about Himself through the Word and creation. In our schedules, as with all our lives, we must become loving and prayerful learners—surrendered to Him, open to His ways, allowing Him to bring all things into His eternal focus.

In God's good time—not yours, and not mine.

## Time Out

• Discuss or journal the notion that time is "God's original, intangible artwork, framed only by day and night."

• Finish the statement, "Time is a gift in my life because . . ."

• Finish the statement, "I struggle with thinking I own my time because . . ."

• How is the ability to steward your time one of the greatest gifts God has given you?

• Stewards have responsibilities. What is your responsibility to God as a steward of the time He has given you? List five ways you can honor God with your time.

• List at least three practical strategies for reminding yourself of God's perspective on time.

# 2

# Everyone Wants to Direct:

## Moving From Hurry to Holy

"All the world's a stage, and all the men and women merely players."

I've always loved that William Shakespeare quote. The whole analogy of life and the theater connects with me because for ten years I taught theater arts to school-age children. I relished directing end-of-the-year productions, especially the adapted Shakespeare play our fifth graders would tackle every spring.

Fifth graders doing Shakespeare—you'd be surprised how well they did it. I was always astounded at how these modern children handled the Elizabethan-era language. They managed not only to pronounce the words and memorize their lines but also, with coaching, to add the appropriate inflection and action. However, I found the students still needed a few reminders. The necessary reminders consisted of projecting their volume and slowing down the speed of dialogue delivery.

The speeding part was the most difficult problem. It stemmed from the fact that although the students knew their lines, when they felt anxious (worrying that they would drop lines), they sped up. And when they did, of course, they became unintelligible. So my constant plea was, "Slow down your words!"

# The Time of Your Life

**A person who moves too quickly may go the wrong way. (Proverbs 19:2, NLT)**

I believe that anxiety does the same thing to most of us in our daily lives. It speeds us up. It makes slowing down really hard. And it brings a lot of confusion into our lives.

We're not so much concerned that we'll forget the dialogue of our lives. We're afraid we won't be able to get through the play at all. We're so anxious to accomplish all we want to do and all we think we're supposed to do that we tend to go faster and faster. We hurry to get the kids off to school, we hurry to our jobs, and we hurry home again—only to start over again in the morning. It's as if some director in the backs of our minds is yelling, "Hurry, hurry, hurry."

And it's not just that way with individuals—it's our whole culture. We are a nation of *very busy people*, and we've been that way since the very beginning. It was Thomas Jefferson, after all, who exhorted us "never to be idle. No person will have occasion to complain of the want of time who never loses any. It is wonderful how much can be done if we are always doing."[1] And it was Benjamin Franklin who originated the phrase "Time is money" and told us that "if time be of all things the most precious, wasting time must be the greatest prodigality."

The fever of busyness, in other words, can be traced to our forefathers' earliest thoughts. We have truly taken their ideas to heart. And while, obviously, this "get it done" creed has helped us accomplish a lot as a nation, I believe it has also left us in want—in want of time, in want of peace, in want of rest.

Most people I know want a little more time and a little less busyness. We blink, the year has passed, and we're still answering, "How are you doing?" with the same response: "Tired and busy." Aren't you ready for a change?

Getting more time and being less busy requires having a personal schedule planner who has knowledge of the future. We are in need of a life coach who can preview our days and help plan them with us. We need more dependence on someone with greater perspective—the perspective of who we are and what we need and where our time is best spent.

Plainly, we need more God in our schedule.
We need more God in our planning.
We need more God.

**He orders our days to be sure. . . . In some strange way, when we are about his business, he makes the eternity about which we know so very little work in our favor. (Karen Mains)**

More specifically, we need to allow God to fulfill His self-appointed role as the director of our lives. On the stage, a director is one who supervises the production of a show and takes responsibility for its outcome. When God is Director of your life, He is the one who supervises the whole production, from start to finish. He is the one who takes full responsibility for your life.

He willingly died for the privilege. And though I do love the Shakespearean quote that opened this chapter, the truth is that in life we are not *merely* players. If we were *merely* players, God wouldn't have needed to take such drastic steps in His answer to our life's ultimate dilemma.

And just what is our ultimate life dilemma? Our eternal existence with or without God. You see, as critical as it is to spend time well on earth, it is equally important to realize that you will exist eternally because you are made in the likeness of God, with an invisible soul. And honestly, apart from everyday time issues, we are a people in need of a Savior because the Bible clearly states that our best attempts to please God will never measure up. Romans 3:23 tells us that we have all sinned, we've all messed up our lives one way or another. And as a result, we are in need of a sacrifice to cover the blunders and failings. So God steps in with His answer: Jesus Christ. Jesus is the answer to your everyday issues and the answer to your ultimate life dilemma: life with or without God for all time, throughout eternity. God made a sacrifice because He earnestly desires to be not only the Director of your life here on earth but the Savior of your entire being forever.

# The Time of Your Life

*For God so loved the world, that he gave his only Son, that whoever*
*believes in him should not perish but have eternal life. For God did not*
*send his Son into the world to condemn the world, but in order that the*
*world might be saved through him. (John 3:16-17)*

*That* is a director who is interested in your life. His love for you led
Him to a dramatic sacrifice. And while that sacrifice, upon your acceptance of it, allows for the final act of your life to open and end in heaven,
it has implications for your scenes here on earth as well.

God's approach, you see, is quite different from that of the hurry-
up culture around us. He is not leading the heavenly choir in a rousing
version of "Hurry, hurry, hurry," hoping you'll hear and speed things up
a bit. Instead, if you listen carefully, you might hear the awe-inspiring
strains of "Holy, Holy, Holy."

That's what God the Director wants for your life.

Not a life of hurry but a life of *holy*.

*Holy* means set apart. It means devoted entirely to God and His
work in your life. The apostle Paul explained it this way: "I appeal to
you therefore, brothers, by the mercies of God to present your bodies
as a living sacrifice, *holy* and acceptable to God, which is your spiritual
worship" (Romans 12:1).

But *holy* sounds elusive, otherworldly, downright impossible—and
frankly, it *is* impossible. We cannot make it happen by ourselves. But
we do become holy when we are touched and consecrated by One who
is holy. And that can only happen when we allow God to be the
Director in our lives.

Have you ever read or seen interviews in which actors talk about
directors they truly love and admire? The best directors don't just tell
actors what to do. They take responsibility for the whole atmosphere
of the play. They stay in close touch with the players and influence them
with their vision. They help actors become the characters they are trying to be.

There's a certain sacrifice that actors must make to work with such
a director. Perhaps they must give up set ideas about how a scene
should work. Or perhaps they need to follow direction even when it
doesn't make sense to them. Sometimes they have to give up their juici-

est scenes or favorite lines in the interest of the director's vision. But their reward is to become part of something bigger and more wonderful than anything they could do on their own. And that's the way it works in life too. The only way to get *holy* is to present yourself to the Holy One and let Him act upon you. You present yourself as *wholly* available, and He connects with you through the gift of Jesus Christ. Every day and in every way, you submit to God as the Director of your life, even when such submission feels like a sacrifice of what you would like to do. And as you do that, you are made holy through His presence.

C. S. Lewis writes:

> For He claims all, because He is love and must bless. He cannot bless us unless He has us. When we try to keep within us an area that is our own, we try to keep an area of death. Therefore, in love, He claims all. There's no bargaining with Him.[2]

What does all this have to do with time and hurry? It's really quite simple: a play can only have one director. And when we accept God as our Director, we have to listen to His voice above all others—including the worries and anxieties and cultural pressures that keep us tired and busy.

He's the one in charge. And He won't bargain with us regarding our time, though it remains for us to choose. His coaching is always, "Slow down. Listen to me. Let me guide you."

**The heart that is to be filled to the brim with holy joy must be held still. (George Seaton Bowes)**

While the world esteems being busy and in a hurry, would you consider esteeming holiness in your everyday life? Include God in practical ways as the Director of your life. Ask Him to open your eyes to His will for your daily life, your script for the day. Try yielding all the small pieces of your day to Him, realizing He moves you here and there across the stage of your life. Allow Him to guide your interaction with other characters who share the stage with you, even the people you would rather avoid.

Consider that God is interested in your audience as well—for your sake and His. He wants it apparent to anyone who cares to pay attention that He's the One in the Director's chair. It's He who appoints your every move and every mood. Not your job, not your hobbies, not your toys, not our frantic, hurried culture but God.

Your enjoyment of life hinges on handing it all over.

Do you want less tiredness? Let God manage it.

Do you want less busyness? He will move you from hurry to holy.

And when He does, you'll be surprised how well you do.

## Time Out

• How often are you in a hurry during your day? Try tallying how many times you hurry yourself or someone else daily. Afterward, consider what percentage of your day you are hurrying. In other words, how much hurry is in your day?

• Describe a typical day filled with hurry.

• Describe a day filled with holy. When in your life have you experienced such a day?

• Identify the key difference between a day filled with hurry and a day filled with holy.

• If a casual acquaintance could peer into your life, who or what would they identify as the driving focus of your life? Who or what would be identified as your personal director?

• What sacrifices do you fear you might have to make if you seriously saw God as the Director of your life? What practical benefits can you see?

• What practical steps can you take every day to make yourself available to God as your Director?

# 3

## Insufficient Funds:

### The Solution to an Overdrawn Life

**The first and only time** my teenaged son was overdrawn on his checking account was when he was out running around and needed gas for his truck. Knowing he was nearing a zero balance, he used his debit card to put in just seven dollars' worth and some change. Then he came home and discovered he had overestimated his balance—by thirty-two cents. A mere thirty-two cents had pushed his account into the red—for which the bank charged him thirty-five dollars! That penalty for "insufficient funds" was about a hundred times more than the error.

*Insufficient* is another word for inadequate. *Funds* means supply. The problem was inadequate supply. That's how we often feel about our own life, isn't it? And often we find we're overdrawn by much more than a few pennies—or a few moments. We're way in the red when it comes to time, and we have no idea what to do about it.

I wonder at my own feelings of inadequate supply. As I look at the bank account of my personal life, I should feel like the richest woman in the world. I accepted Christ at twelve. I grew up in a Christian family. I married my high-school sweetheart, and we have three awesome kids. My husband pastors a church we founded, and we live in the great city of Austin, Texas, where we grew up. A bevy of loving people surrounds us, including both sets of parents. And yet sometimes, truly many times, I struggle with the sense that I just don't have enough or that I will quickly exhaust my supply of what I need. And when I feel the insufficiency deep within, I end up feeling pretty bad about myself. I can be doing the very best I can and yet find myself feeling just like my son—overdrawn and definitely feeling the penalty.

There is probably no area that reflects this sense of deficit in my life like that of my time. It's a daily and delicate balance to keep my time account in the black. Nightly I scan my house, noticing the various things that didn't get done that day and are waiting for me tomorrow. They are always there. And so I find myself teetering on the brink of an overdraft, my stomach tight with the tension of not having enough time to get everything done.

Philippians 4:19 states, "My God will supply every need of yours according to his riches in glory in Christ Jesus." If you find yourself looking at a day bursting full of demands, perhaps you're like me and would love for God to provide those riches in the form of a few more hours in your day.

**Here is a simple revelation that is bringing me a lot of freedom: There is enough time. . . . I am discovering that I have exactly the right number of hours and minutes and seconds to accomplish and do everything that I need to do in my lifetime. (Claire Cloninger)**

A friend posed a question recently: "What would you do if you had a twenty-eight-hour day instead of a twenty-four-hour one?" I can tell you my immediate thought was, "I would get caught up!" The fact that I constantly feel behind in my day seems to imply that I somehow have an inadequate supply of the thing I need: time. Many women I know feel the same way. We are fully involved with the crazy details of our life. All too often, though, we're overspent, and the penalty for being overdrawn seems to be about a hundred times more than the overdraft.

Time is the most valued commodity in our culture. We wish for more time for ourselves and those we love so we can live the life we envision. But sadly, it seems ever beyond our grasp. In many ways we are a spent society. Anjula Razdan expresses this feeling eloquently:

> Lately, I've been approaching bedtime the way, I assume, marathoners approach the finish line, which is to say, exhausted and in need of a nourishing IV. Buoyed by the frenetic pace of what philosophy professor Al Gini has called "the Everydayathon" of modern life, I leapfrog from errand to errand, desperate to get my unwieldy to-do list under control. No longer do I have time in my overbooked life for the kind of roomy, deep-focus activities that used to sustain me. The bookcase behind my bed is a shrine to my aborted attempts at reading novels, my e-mail box a painful reminder of the nurturing friendships I've let drift away. I even have a slow cooker I've never used.[1]

Can you relate? I certainly can. Let me confess that I broke down and purchased an espresso machine because I found that my "nourishing IV" is a cappuccino twice a day. Now I don't "leapfrog" from errand to errand; instead, I charge like a thoroughbred on a racetrack, gnawing at the bit, foaming at the mouth. My "roomy, deep-focus activities" consist of folding laundry while catching up on a modest share of mindless TV. We all have our little ways of getting through our "Everydayathon."

Literally thousands of people, for example, will willingly pay just to have a few more hours in their day. Just today I found a flyer on my doorstep advertising a lawn-maintenance service. The copy read, "What is your weekend worth?" On the inside of the flyer was a pricing schedule for the service. It looked really good—so good in fact that if we didn't already have someone helping us with our lawn, I would have surely called them.

We pay for help with our yards, with our houses, with our children. We simply can't get it all done, and we happily compensate people for taking over the excess in our lives. And that's not a bad solution, really, except it doesn't fix the problem for long. Spent to deprivation, we still have insufficient time to get through our daily life. Or so it seems. So we churn on, coffee or cola in hand, to the next appointment, the next chore, spurred on by the never-ending chiding of the clock and our own inner turmoil.

That turmoil sends us, frantic, in search of guidance. We consult all manner of "experts" who tell us it's all a matter of efficiency, of finding better ways to whip our hours into shape. We gladly pay to listen to these gurus expound on better ways to slice and dice our calendars—and pay again, months later, when our lives aren't getting better. But all too often we neglect to consult the Creator of time Himself. His authoritative guide to time remains stacked silently on the shelf.

And that, of course, is the real problem.

Before we can begin to find answers to our overdrawn time accounts, I think we must first come to grasp the possibility that the answer is not just more hours in our day—or even better organization of the hours we have. Certainly everyone can benefit from increased efficiency and extra help, but that only addresses the outward part of the issue. As with a person who overspends financially, getting more money to cover the deficit is not a satisfactory solution—because it does nothing to teach a person how to spend well or stay out of debt.

To keep a balance in the black, spending habits and spending motivations must be examined. The same is true for the overly busy, the tired, and the time-deprived. Internal habits and motivations need to be examined, and these may require a serious look in light of biblical principles. And while that might sound a little painful, I have some really great news: You can balance your life account and live in the black. God wants that for you. He'll even supply the necessary funds.

Think of that. What if I told you that someone at your bank was interested in providing an ongoing supply of resources for your account—for free? No service charge, no interest. You'd be skeptical, I bet, just like me. But if you are curious about the biblical reality, I must tell you that it is true in regard to your schedule. God has a lifestyle of positive balance in mind where your time is concerned. He intends for you to have rest and joy and pleasure in abundance. And He will give you what you need to make it happen. Enough of everything. Even time.

The book of Ecclesiastes tells us that God "has made everything beautiful in its time" and that "there is nothing better for [human beings] than to be joyful and to do good as long as they live; also that everyone should eat and drink and take pleasure in all his toil—this is God's gift to man" (3:11-13).

**The problem, of course, is that many of us multi-tasking women have reached the point that we just can't do much more. Even if we could, our nervous systems couldn't take the strain. So many of us are burned out. We are falling behind. Because we've allowed our sense of self-worth to be connected with how much we cram into a day, we're feeling worse and worse. And because we take our information in sound bites and have little time to devote to deeper things, we are in danger of becoming shallow and superficial. (Donna Otto)**

Living a depleted lifestyle, in other words, was never what God had in mind for you. The constraints and frustrations you continually feel are not the result of God's lack of provision. He is a God of sufficiency, able to supply all your needs in Jesus Christ. He is not wringing His hands in heaven wondering how He can send some emergency help on your behalf. He is fully able to supply you with more than what you need. Even better, He has provided you with a life-sized role model for wise spending:

> *For we do not have a high priest who is unable to sympathize with our weaknesses, but one who in every respect has been tempted as we are, yet without sin. Let us then with confidence draw near to the throne of grace, that we may receive mercy and find grace to help in time of need.* (Hebrews 4:15-16)

Jesus lived an earthly life as a man, remember, and He certainly had a load of things to accomplish. No doubt He went to bed at night and wondered about how it would all get done. And yet He never griped about His job or His lack of time. He did not squander His time or energy; instead He beautifully succeeded in accomplishing the job set before Him. And although He surely felt the weakness associated with living a busy life, He was without sin. This is our sympathetic priest, our ultimate role model, the man who lived a life of complete but unhurried efficiency, leaning on the Father for all sufficiency.

Even now, Jesus looks down on your overdrawn, overspent life and desires to show you a better way. So the first place to go with your insanely busy days, your out-of-balance schedule, is to His throne of grace.

You'll never be overdrawn if you make the choice to rely on His abundant provision.

## Time Out

• Describe your personal "Everydayathon."

• Which activities in your life tend to create insufficient funds where your time is concerned? How would you describe the penalty you pay for the negative time balance?

• If your best friend were to ask you today, "How are you doing?" what would be your honest answer? What if she asked, "How balanced is your schedule?"

• What time experts have you gone to, attempting to order your life more effectively? What advice has actually helped you?

# 4

# Patients:

## God's Prescription for Our Hurry Sickness

**I made sure not only** to be on time but to arrive early at the doctor's office. Clearly this was my first mistake—to assume that somehow my promptness would mysteriously mandate the doctor's running on schedule.

After checking in and watching thirty minutes tick away, I went to the front desk to inquire about when my name would be called. The receptionist smiled sweetly and told me that the doctor had just stepped back in from delivering a baby and was now beginning to see his regular patients. I smiled back tersely, picked up another worn magazine, and noted the packed waiting room.

After a full hour had slipped away, I stared at the front desk hoping they would sense my impatient disgust. The office personnel chattered away, oblivious. Finally, when I could stand it no more, I stalked up to the desk. "How long will it be before Dr. Johnson is able to see me?" The receptionist looked startled.

"Oh, let me check, Mrs. Davis." She checked. "It appears there is only one more patient in front of you."

"And then I will be seen?" I questioned.

"Yes." She smiled back warmly. "Then it will be your turn."

I sat back down again to wait. And wait. And to tell myself that as much as I wanted to be understanding, I had been pushed too far. There was really no stopping me from saying *something* to *somebody* about the ridiculousness of the time I had already spent in the waiting room. I imagined telling the doctor sarcastically that it must be just *awful* always to be running behind. I eyed the survey form and imagined writing something very clever but *very* pointed to alert the doctor about the lax attitude concerning an hour-long wait. But just as quickly as the thought was birthed, I was called back to a room.

The nurse asked all the customary questions. I answered in quick sentences, my arms folded. I wasn't rude, but I wasn't exactly gracious either. This office had wasted my time; I hadn't heard anything that sounded remotely like an apology. And frankly, I was steamed. Although I knew that the doctor had been called out to deliver a baby, which was not only his job but outside of his control, I still felt angry and impatient. Those minutes I'd just spent waiting on him were precious to me. It was the time in my day meant for running errands, meeting a friend for lunch, catching up on household chores. I really had no desire to spend my precious time cooling my heels in a doctor's waiting room.

I was led to an examination room and found myself sitting at the end of a cold, clinical table. I felt angry, impatient, and somewhat fragile in the insubstantial cotton robe. There was a quick knock at the door, and the doctor breezed in with the nurse behind him. "Mrs. Davis!" he exclaimed, giving me a quick hug around the shoulder, "It's been a while. How are you?"

I was taken back by his tenderness and his hug, but still a little miffed, mind you. But there was his face, smiling, encouraging me to speak.

"I'm fine." I finally stuttered.

"Well, what can we do for you today?" he asked. "Just a physical?"

"Yes," I replied. "Just a physical."

**By replanning our lives around his values we can learn that "hurry sickness" is not meant to be our inevitable end. We can live peacefully and in harmony with God's purposes. (Dr. Archibald Hart)**

## Patients:
## God's Prescription For Our Hurry Sickness

After I had endured the poking and prodding that always accompany a physical, he stood to leave and gave me *another* friendly hug. And as he left the room I realized I was smiling. Not because he gave me what I thought I wanted, which was my lost time back—or an apology for taking it away, but because he saw me as I was, arms folded and impatient, and gave me what I really needed, which was a physician's healing touch.

God sees me like that in so many situations of my life—arms folded, toe tapping, irritated and impatient. And He sees you that way too. He sees how we are trying to hold it all together. He looks at our life in this grand waiting room, sometimes trying hard to be nice, sometimes falling apart. He knows all those cranky little thoughts rolling around in our heads, the ungenerous words we'd like to say—or *do* say—when people or situations put a damper on our plans. Even our secret little assumptions that God Himself could do a better job of managing His universe (especially in regard to our personal lives).

And God knows what we so often fail to realize.

We may think we need more time for ourselves. But what we really need is time with the One who knows us better than we know ourselves. We need God's guidance, His personal and healing touch.

And He is very willing to meet us where we are, whatever our attitude or our demeanor. As a matter of fact, if you feel tired and empty or impatient, I have fabulous news: The Doctor is in for you. Always.

God is the great Physician, the Healer of your life and times. In all the places of your life that you find need—including your time issues— He is more than able to provide. As you seek to gain perspective and balance in the area of your life known as your time, realize that He's the One who holds the prescription for all the negative influences infecting your life. He would love to wrap His arms around your weary days and bring you to wellness and real life.

And yes, sometimes it seems that God is the One who keeps you waiting, that your prayers go unanswered and your problems go unsolved and you just can't feel His presence. But God, after all, operates on His time schedule and not ours. He sees the big picture, and though He doesn't take orders from us, He always gets there right on time. Best of all, He brings His healing presence, which is what we really need.

# The Time of Your Life

Not more time.

Not more hours in the day.

But healing for our hurried hearts and minds and bodies so that we can make the best use of the time we have.

And make no mistake. Hurry can indeed be a sickness—or at least a symptom. It's a recognized syndrome, a contributor to all sorts of physical and emotional ailments—from anxiety to strokes to heart disease. If you look around, you will see that most of us drive ourselves beyond capacity. And our symptoms are spiritual as well. As people race about, they despair over their inability to manage life, feeling overwhelmed.

Like many people with physical ailments, though, we tend to be more interested in a quick fix than we are in a real cure. We just want to make things easier. So we pin our hopes on cell phones, Palm Pilots, day planners, efficiency experts, professional organizers, life coaches. We hope they'll patch us up, make quick sense of our crammed schedules. But all our scheming just leaves us more desperate. Will we finally, exhausted, seek the Doctor who has the capacity to do something significant with our lives and our time?

He's going to do it His own way, though. And that's important to realize, because sometimes we're guilty of looking to God for the same kind of quick fix we demand from the efficiency experts. We send up quick prayers for Him to ease the knots in our schedules or our stomachs, to iron out the problems our own hurry has caused. And God, in His mercy, often answers these prayers. (He's done it for me.) But He may well have something else in mind for us, something we don't even know we need.

In the Gospel of Mark we meet a woman who experienced this with Jesus. Like us, this woman was desperate for a cure. She too had sought the experts. She too had spent all she had seeking a cure for her symptoms, but she had just grown worse. Then she heard of a hope, and that hope was Jesus:

*She had heard the report about Jesus and came up behind him in the crowd and touched his garment. For she said, "If I touch even his garments, I will be made well." (5:27-28)*

## Patients:
## God's Prescription For Our Hurry Sickness

In the depths of her despair, that woman was willing to secretly reach for Jesus. Inside her soul she muttered a prayer, and the Bible tells us that at once her physical problem ceased. The bleeding of twelve years stopped. But that was not enough for Jesus.

*And Jesus, perceiving in himself that power had gone out from him, immediately turned about in the crowd and said, "Who touched my garments?" And his disciples said to him, "You see the crowd pressing around you, and yet you say, 'Who touched me?'" And he looked around to see who had done it. But the woman, knowing what had happened to her, came in fear and trembling and fell down before him and told him the whole truth. And he said to her, "Daughter, your faith has made you well; go in peace, and be healed of your disease." (vv. 30-34)*

I have always wondered why Jesus asked who had touched Him when He surely knew. Why did His eyes scan the jostling crowd? Why did He look patiently here and there, gently ignoring the disciples who surely spoke with reason? Why create tension and discomfort for the poor woman, who probably just wanted to be healed and go on her way?

I think it's the same reason God makes us wait sometimes, why He seemingly lets our prayers for help go unanswered. You see, it is never enough for Him simply to solve our problems. He desires not only to heal us but also to be with us.

Jesus waited for the woman to acknowledge His question because He honestly desired to see her face, to acknowledge her pain, to heal her body and her soul, to encourage her spirit. He allowed the discomfort because He *loved* her. And because He had something even more lavish to do with her than ease her symptoms. He wanted to make her *whole*.

Does God want to help you with your schedule? Does He desire for you to be healed of your hurry sickness, your fretful lifestyle, and your onerous to-do list?

Yes, of course.

But not at the expense of missing Him.

He will never settle for giving you something good when He can give you something better. He will never hand out a prescription without your understanding how to spend your wellness.

**43**

# The Time of Your Life

**Love cures people—both the ones who give it and the ones who receive it. (Dr. Karl Menninger)**

Jesus told the woman, "Your faith has made you well." Our faith can make us well too, but that's just the start of what the Great Physician wants for us. Why fix a schedule outside of Him?

If your schedule has driven you to your knees, why not go the whole distance—to His feet? Why not fall down before Him and tell Him the whole truth? I am quite sure He will look into your face and lift your eyes to His, loving you all the while.

Do not seek wellness outside of His will. You will become sick again. Take the time to let your desperation drive you to needing Him and loving Him. Let the tension, the discomfort, have its place. That kind of tension in life, the kind that draws you back to neediness again and again, is just the thing Jesus wants. He asks us to be continually dependent upon Him, seeking Him first in everything.

I honestly do not know if my long wait for my doctor could have been avoided, but I do know that my visit with him changed the direction of my day. And I do not know if just a touch from Jesus would have kept the woman from bleeding again, but I know her time with Him changed her life.

If you are tired of running your life and find yourself spending all your time and money on the wrong doctors, it's time to turn to the One who can really heal you. Fall at His feet, look in His face, and see the gracious eyes of God on your tired, worn soul. Give Him your impatience, your irritation, your stress, and your worry. He is waiting, ever patient, allowing the tension to grow and expand your need of Him in this life.

Meet the God of all time and space—the Great Physician of *your* time and space. He is ready and willing to prescribe His plan for your wellness. If your hurry sickness has brought you to this point, I am so grateful for the problem because you are going to get far more than you ever hoped for— a life worth living and a life worth giving, managed by the Healer and Lover of your soul.

God is giving you today—in His good time.

## Time Out

• When in your day are you typically most cranky and irritable? Why?

• One evening this week, sit down and contemplate a typical day. How many times in a day are you impatient with others? With situations?

• What is the most common emotion you experience when you feel impatient?

• What is the most habitual action you take when you are impatient?

• If God could catch you on your cell phone at the most impatient moments of your day, what would you guess He might say to you?

• Find a verse that adequately communicates what your Great Physician would say concerning your tendency to become impatient. Consider inputting the reference on your cell phone or Palm Pilot or on a note card as a reminder of what God has to say about your impatient moments.

# 5

# Moments That Matter:

## What God Wants Most From You

**It was an evening** I had been anticipating for months. Will, my son, was graduating from high school.

We had arrived early at the church where the ceremony was to take place to ensure that we could secure the perfect seat near the aisle. We had fresh batteries in the video camera. I was ready.

I watched carefully through the camera lens as the procession began. As each student filed by me, I felt more excitement. Suddenly, as if by coincidence, a familiar face entered the viewfinder. I lifted my eye from the camera, and there he was, my firstborn and my only son, Will Davis III. Tears trickled down my cheeks as I fixed my attention on that beloved face. For a brief moment our eyes met, and then he strolled confidently past, disappearing into the rows and rows of young men and women in red caps and gowns.

What a moment that was.

But as I watched, I found myself thinking back to all the other moments in our lives that had led up to that one. Bedtime stories and toy trains and planes. Endless carpooling. Massive homework sessions. Family dinners and lots of laughter. Occasional terse words (his and mine). Deep God conversations and ministry musings. Some moments were beautiful. Some were ugly. Some were easy and some hard. Some

I wished would last forever, and some I hoped to wish away. But none of those moments could be traded because they were the pieces of our togetherness. The moments added up to a relationship that is unutterably beautiful to me. I love my son.

And then I thought, what if I hadn't had those moments with Will? What if I had let all the busyness of my life overwhelm my schedule so that I had never really known him or made him a priority? I would have said with my life that I never cared to be with him, that I wasn't truly interested in who he was or what mattered to him. I would have failed to tangibly express my love for him if I hadn't spent time knowing him. Delighting in him as he played his guitar, leading worship. Laughing with him over a game of Nerts. Knowing all his favorites, from Wendy's to homemade sourdough bread.

It would grieve me deeply if my son left for college feeling I had never spent time with him. Imagine spending a lifetime as a mother without ever really knowing your child. To me, that would be unbearable. And yet isn't that the mistake we often make with God?

Our relationship with Him is very much like my relationship with my son—it is made up of little moments. And those moments matter. They matter to us, and they matter to God.

**Let us remember that the life in which we ought to be interested is "daily" life. We can, each of us, call only the present time our own. (St. Gregory of Nyssa)**

Too often, I think, we tend to view life in terms of starts and finishes and big transitions. Perhaps it is our compulsion with graduating on to the next thing. We anxiously await the next job, the next season, or whatever is considered the next big milestone. But all too often while we are looking ahead, we are missing the little moments that make up our lives right now.

Though you have often heard it said, it bears repeating: The most important day on your calendar wasn't yesterday and it isn't tomorrow—it's today. Today is the most important day you have because it is the only day you have. And yes, you've heard that too. But knowing something and living its reality aren't the same thing at all. Today is the day to take those small moments and give them to those you care about, including God.

Especially God.

Do you allow God to have pieces and moments of your today? According to the Bible, He is looking for you: "God looks down from heaven on the children of man to see if there are any who understand, who seek after God" (Psalm 53:2). But perhaps you feel there are no moments left in your day for Him, that you are totally spent from taking care of everyone else and everything else, or that what few moments you have left over aren't really enough to count.

But that's not the way the Lord looks at it. He treasures whatever we have to give Him, however small. And He especially appreciates our efforts to give Him what we have out of whatever we currently possess. In Luke 21:1-4 we find the familiar story of a woman who did just that.

> *Jesus looked up and saw the rich putting their gifts into the offering box, and he saw a poor widow put in two small copper coins. And he said, "Truly, I tell you, this poor widow has put in more than all of them. For they contributed out of their abundance, but she out of her poverty put in all she had to live on."*

To Jesus, the widow's small copper coins amounted to much more than all the other gifts. That's because she gave sacrificially, contributing out of her poverty. She gave God "all she had to live on," though it was very small. And that act of giving spoke eloquently of what she really valued. Ken Gire writes in *Windows of the Soul*,

> The widow had nothing to live on and no one to look after her. Her concern wasn't a mortgage payment; it was her next meal. That's why the offering was so extraordinary. The fraction of a cent represented the focus of her life. It represented not only her faithfulness in helping to provide for God's work but also her faith in God to provide.[1]

You've probably heard the story of the widow and her coins a million times. But have you ever considered what that story has to tell you about your time, about the moments of your life? Maybe you feel that no one is looking after you, helping you, in regard to your schedule. Your heartfelt concern is literally getting through the day, taking care of all the needs screaming for your attention, in the amount of time you have. You are as worn-out as she was, with barely enough reserve to get by. Is your first instinct to do as she did—to give what little you can to God? Or are you tempted to hold on to what you have, to hoard your few remaining minutes and use them for yourself?

I suspect I know the answer for most of us. We would love to spend more time with God . . . if we just had the time to spend. Besides, a moment here and there isn't enough. Shouldn't we just wait until we have time to go on a retreat or join a Bible study? Then we could really get serious about spending time with God.

**Every day has its own particular brand of holiness to discover and worship appropriately. (Annie Dillard)**

But as the widow's story indicates, God doesn't look at things that way. Whether we are rich or poor in time or money, Jesus treasures our offering. He wants whatever we can give Him *today*. He's not seeking to bleed us dry, to take from us what we don't have. He just knows that when we give sacrificially, we're getting serious about what matters most in life. In a sense we are investing in a relationship with God—an investment that always pays dividends in terms of real fulfillment and meaning.

What does all this mean in a practical sense? Simply that conquering your calendar woes has a lot to do with making God a priority in your life. Having time is all about giving God time before He gets shoved out by other demands. C. S. Lewis recommends that we do just that:

> It comes the very moment you wake up each morning. All your wishes and hopes for the day rush at you like wild animals. And the first job each morning consists simply in shoving them all back; in listening to that other voice, taking that other point of view, letting

that other larger, stronger, quieter life come flowing back in. And so on, all day. Standing back from all your natural fussings and frettings; coming in out of the wind.[2]

I don't know about you, but I feel those wild animals rush at me all day long. And I find I am continually shoving them back. I often muse aloud that God called me into the ministry because He knew I would be so distracted without the vocational commitment. I seem to have much fussing and fretting. For me, "coming in out of the wind" is a moment-to-moment battle. And so I pray and ask in a daily way, often before my feet touch the floor in the morning, that I will be able to love God with all my energy that day. I recognize I need all the help from Him I can get. I even need His help to love Him more.

It's possible to spend a lifetime as a "Christian" and yet never really know God—because we manage to leave Him out of our schedule. Moment by moment, He gets pushed back, and the days become months and the months years, and we have yet to delight in Him, to laugh with Him when He manifests humor in our life, to know His favorites, like obedience and mercy, to spend moment to moment with Him as Savior, Lord, and Friend.

What kind of grief does He bear, loving us as He does and yet being excluded from our lives, knowing that we long for peace, that our real peace comes in spending time with Him, that our schedules are healed and made right only through His wisdom, but that we refuse to make that time a priority? It really only takes a small step toward Him, a moment or two set aside in a day, to keep going in the right direction. When we give sacrificially of our moments, God is faithful to build on that investment.

And yet we still make our excuses. We don't have time for God because we don't make time for God. And how we suffer as a result. Our ignorance makes us orphans. Our busyness leaves us bereft. And all the while we are just one small step away from the quiet confidence of knowing and being known by God *today*. No wonder the writer of Hebrews urged his brothers and sisters to "exhort one another every day, as long as it is called 'today,' that none of you may be hardened by the deceitfulness of sin" (3:13)—or even by the perception of a calendar too packed for God.

God does not look at your life and cheer you on to the big win. He has already taken care of that for you. He's not there just for those big transitional moments like birth and death. Instead He looks on your life today, yearning to spend those small moments with you.

Day upon day, all in a lifetime, adds up to a lifetime of devotion.

## Time Out

• What are you anxiously looking forward to that might cause you to miss living the moment you are in?

• In what specific ways do you typically seek God in the moments of your day? In what ways could you use your moments better?

• Specifically identify how much you resemble the poor widow in terms of your personal resources. At this particular point in your life, what kinds of poverty do you face?

• Consider the very small moments in your day that are available to spend as you wish. Write down specific time frames, even in increments of a few moments. Think of those as available gifts, and prayerfully consider giving God some of those moments.

• Reread the C. S. Lewis quote. What are the "wishes and hopes" that rush at you when you awake in the morning? How are they like wild animals keeping you from a "larger, stronger, quieter" life?

# 6

# DiVine SaVings Time:

## Springing Forward with God's Energy Plan

**Did you know that** Benjamin Franklin invented daylight savings time?

He didn't specifically call it that. And he didn't exactly come up with the idea of springing forward and falling back. But way back in 1784 Benjamin Franklin thought so much of maximizing time and saving energy that he proposed changing society's habits to take advantage of available sunshine.

The idea was birthed when Franklin, who was serving as ambassador to Paris, awoke to find he had "wasted" precious daylight sleeping. He realized that his habit of working (and playing chess) late into the night, which required him to burn candles in order to see, was less efficient than getting up earlier so he could do more in the daylight. Sunshine, after all, was free—the candles were not. So Franklin wrote an essay in the *Journal de Paris* called "An Economical Project" in which he expounded the superiority of natural versus artificial lighting. He also had some bright things to say about the city's inefficient, expensive use of time and energy.

I say it is impossible that so sensible a people, under such circumstances, should have lived so long by the smoky, unwholesome, and enormously expensive light of candles, if they had really known, that they might have had as much pure light of the sun for nothing.[1]

Now, while it does take a stretch of the imagination to go back and picture what it was really like to light up a house by candlelight, just think of what happens when your electricity pops off in a thunderstorm at night and you are left fumbling for candles. Imagine if the candles available were the kind your eighteenth-century ancestors used: tallow candles. Made from animal fat, these candles burned quickly, rapidly absorbing into the wick and producing black, sooty smoke. Talk about air quality control; there is really no modern comparison for the filth of the tallow candle. And to top it off, tallow candles were expensive, and there was there a tax on them. But they were the standard synthetic light source in Franklin's day.

No wonder Franklin lobbied for an alternative resource: sunshine. Free. Beautiful. Wholesome. "Pure light of the sun for nothing" is the way Franklin put it. Smart man, that Franklin. He understood a fundamental and life-changing reality: making the best use of time is really a matter of using energy well.

The citizens of Paris never took Benjamin Franklin's idea seriously. (He actually recommended that all the bells of the city be rung at daylight to make sure everyone got out of bed.) It took several centuries, a world war, and an energy crisis for us to catch up to the revolutionary idea of rearranging the hours to make use of available sunlight. Even now, when springing forward and falling back is the law in most states, the idea still has its detractors—even I sometimes balk at it.

## For this I toil, struggling with all his [God's] energy that he powerfully works within me. (Colossians 1:29)

Oh, it's great in the fall. I savor the feeling of waking and suddenly realizing I have "gained" an hour. It is not nearly as late as I thought. I am *ahead* of schedule. That is pure luxury in my mind. I feel energetic and ready to face the world with my big head start. Spring, on the other hand, always takes me by surprise. Springing forward makes me feel like my time has been stolen. I lose an hour. I awake that morning in

# Divine Savings Time:
## Springing Forward with God's Energy Plan

April thinking all is well with the world, only to find I am an hour behind schedule.

Daylight savings time can really trip me up—and I've been adjusting to it all my life. Can you imagine the people in Ben Franklin's time even entertaining the notion? It's understandable that they thought the idea preposterous. Change is hard, especially when it affects time and energy.

Now, while daylight savings time is intended to conserve physical resources, whether tallow in the eighteenth century or fossil fuel in our current times, you are most likely interested in making better use of your *personal energy*. You know the kind of energy I mean. It's what gives you the ability to get up and get breakfast started. It's what pushes you forward to take care of your family with all the necessary errands— going to the grocery store, driving the carpools, making meetings, and the like. And what about the relational energy you spend on your husband, your children, your extended family, and your friends? Spending your personal energy wisely is an important concern because every one of us has only so much to spend.

Only so much energy, and only so much time.

Franklin observed in his culture a regrettable waste of time and free energy. Is there a parallel for us? Do we waste time and energy, settling for a sooty tallow candle when there is a free, wholesome alternative available to us? Just as people in Franklin's time had to warm up to his revolutionary thoughts, maybe we need to pull ourselves in for a closer look at some revolutionary thinking about time and energy.

John in the fourth Gospel wrote concerning Jesus:

*In him was life, and the life was the light of men. (1:4)*

*There it was—the true Light [was then] coming into the world [the genuine, perfect, steadfast Light] that illumines every person. (1:9, AMP)*

*Once more Jesus addressed the crowd. He said, I am the Light of the world. He who follows Me will not be walking in the dark, but will have the Light which is Life. (8:12, AMP)*

Jesus' statements about being *the Light* can infiltrate our understanding. As we draw closer to Him, suddenly we can *see*. And then we have *Life*—the kind of life that is full of energy and abundance. It's free for the taking—if we can adjust the way we live in order to take advantage of it.

## Light tomorrow with today. (Elizabeth Barrett Browning)

Jesus Himself said, "I came so they can have real and eternal life, more and better life than they ever dreamed of" (John 10:10, MSG). I want that kind of life. I bet you'd like that too. And we can have it, even down to the way it affects our schedules. The catch is that we have to look to Jesus to understand how to live that kind of life. And when it comes to time and energy expenditure, we also need to understand two key points: how God set up time and how God set up people—both in general and as individuals.

How can we gain that kind of understanding? It's right there in the Creator's handbook. He has unique knowledge of His creation, He has His *will for you* laid out in advance, and He's revealed both of these in the pages of the Bible. To take advantage of His gifts of time and energy, all you really need is to say yes to God and His plans. You spring forward into God's way of doing things, and, with His help, you resist falling back into your old usage patterns.

But doing things God's way isn't always easy. It requires stretching our minds and pushing past our natural inclinations.

We don't naturally grow toward God, you see. My pastor husband puts it this way: "You never drift toward God. The gravitational drift of life is always away from God." As with daylight savings time, it's always easier to fall back. But while drifting and falling backward might feel easier, it does not always make life simpler. It can even be dangerous, especially in spiritual matters. As Proverbs 14:12 tells us, "There is a way that seems right to a man, but its end is the way to death."

But what does all this mean in terms of time and energy? Simply that taking full advantage of God's energy-saving plan may require springing forward into new ways of thinking. It requires an open mind and quite possibly some spiritual concentration. You may need to pull away from your current schedule, spend some time in God's Word, and open your eyes to the age-old but still revolutionary ways that God works with time and energy.

The truth is, every time you choose to live life God's way, you save energy. When you choose to forgive instead of holding a grudge, you free up precious personal energy. When you choose to love instead of hate, you are springing forward into God's purpose and tapping into the power of His love, which in itself is a form of energy. Every time you offer gratitude to God even in the midst of difficult circumstances, you open yourself to His strength and energy for coping with those very circumstances.

Conversely, when you choose to operate outside God's directives in the Word—which is what God calls sin—you waste energy. Interesting thought, isn't it? Activities grounded in selfishness, greed, hatred, or dishonesty are not just wrong—they're also a waste of time. They'll empty you out without filling you up. It just makes sense that doing things God's way is a better use of available energy.

The sun was free for the eighteenth-century man or woman in need of some extra light. (It is still free!) And God has offered Himself as a free energy source as well—in the Person of Jesus, the true "light of the world." When we adapt our lives to His perspective and open our lives to Him, we receive the energy we need to make optimal use of our time.

This is really the perfect solution for sensible people. It will save you from frustrated living, from wasting your precious time and energy on the world's inefficient and deadly ways of living. And as you embrace God's design of time and realize His plan for your energy expenditure, you will be involving yourself in an economical project of enormous proportion—God's.

## Time Out

• What are some practical ways you can save energy in your everyday schedule?

• On a scale of 1 (being very low) and 10 (being very high), rate how much energy you have at the end of your day.

- What are some of your most energy-depleting activities?
- What are some of your most energy-depleting attitudes?
- How might springing forward into God's ways restore your energy depletion issues?
- Can you identify any issues related to drifting spirituality that could be wreaking havoc in your life and schedule? List three ways you might change such a drift.

# 7

# Sabbath Deprivation Disorder:

## Why God Commands Us to Rest

**When Emily, my older daughter,** was just over a year old, she decided that napping was not for her. She was an able toddler, easily popping over the crib rail and helping herself to freedom. And this caused tremendous tension for me, her mother. I gently tried to woo her back into the crib with blankets and pacifiers. I tried to compel her to nap by standing at her bedroom door and shaking my head no if she resisted. I tried soothing music, and still the child would not rest. Something in her active body compelled her to be up and running around.

It was a trying time for both of us. Inevitably she would end up screaming the afternoon away in annoyed exhaustion. Many days I would end up in tears as well.

Finally we moved Emily to a big bed so I could lie down with her during naps. It seemed the only answer. But she still resisted, climbing over me and plopping onto the floor. Finally, because nothing else had worked, I lay down beside her with my arm across her little body, gently holding her in the bed. And that was what finally worked. Soon we were both asleep, completely worn out by our struggle.

To tell the truth, I still feel that way sometimes. Don't you? If you are like me, there are days when you'd really like someone to require that you take a nap. Or maybe you'd just like to call in sick from your life. Maybe you've become so busy that you're like my friend Ellen, who literally calls herself on her cell phone to leave herself messages so she will remember what she needs to do. "I'll have my people call myself" is her half-serious mantra.

Don't you feel that nagging need to keep up so you won't get behind? Charles Hummel's famous phrase "the tyranny of the urgent" is more than an abstract concept for most of us—we live our lives in emergency mode. We're like little hamsters on the exercise wheel, moving as fast as we can to stay in one place. I know there are days when I wish I had a Starbucks IV drip in my car!

It's not that we're not tired. It's just that we just don't know how to get off the wheel. We have the feeling that if we slow down and rest for even a moment, we'll never get what we have to do—or what we want to do—done. So like my little Emily, we just keep pushing and pushing, growing crankier and more irritable by the minute.

If that's true for you, I have some good news and some bad news for you. The bad news is that you may well have SDD: Sabbath Deprivation Disorder. The good news? It's totally curable.

The key to the cure is what God calls a Sabbath. The name literally means "rest." It's His loving provision for our stubborn weariness, our childish determination to keep on going without a break. And it's something He's had in mind for us from the very beginning of creation.

God designed *everything*, remember, in just six days. And then on the seventh, He did what He would later command His people to do. He rested.

*Thus the heavens and the earth were finished, and all the host of them. And on the seventh day God finished his work that he had done, and he rested on the seventh day from all his work that he had done. So God blessed the seventh day and made it holy, because on it God rested from all his work that he had done in creation. (Gen. 2:1-3)*

Have you ever stopped to wonder why God rested after the completion of creation? Sure, creating the heavens and the earth and day and night and plants and animals was a huge job. But God is God, and surely

## Sabbath Deprivation Disorder:
## Why God Commands Us to Rest

He was not really tired. He is all-powerful, all-knowing, and surely all-energy. Why in the world would He need a time out from His work?

As I have read and reread the above section of Scripture aloud, I have come up with a theory. Moses seems to state and restate the obvious—that God rested. And I have come to wonder, with amusement, if that was the very point. It's actually a very motherly read if you read it out loud. God speaks to us as children. The words cycle back and forth gently, in rhythm.

"Finished . . . finished . . . rested . . . rested."

**Rest is not idleness, and to lie sometimes on the grass under the trees on a summer's day, listening to the murmur of the water, or watching the clouds float across the blue sky, is by no means a waste of time. (Lord Avebury)**

Like a patient mother rocking a weary baby, waiting for the child to doze, the verse quietly insists that God rested because that's what God wanted for *us*. Perhaps He knew we would become such a busy, distracted people, so reluctant to rest, that we needed Him to be a role model of rest for us.

I don't know that for certain, of course. But it is curious to me that of all the commandments He would later give to Moses, this is the one that He chose to actually act out.

*Remember the Sabbath day, to keep it holy. Six days you shall labor, and do all your work, but the seventh day is a Sabbath to the LORD your God. On it you shall not do any work, you, or your son, or your daughter, your male servant, or your female servant, or your livestock, or the sojourner who is within your gates. For in six days the LORD made heaven and earth, the sea, and all that is in them, and rested the seventh day. Therefore the LORD blessed the Sabbath day and made it holy. (Exodus 20:8-11)*

It's also interesting to me how detailed this commandment is—it covers more verses than any of the other ten, providing very specific descriptions of who, what, when, and why, just like game rules for beginners. And Moses included *everyone* in his description of Sabbath rest, right down to the livestock and the houseguests.

Why the careful outline? Could this have been the beginning of an eternal infomercial about the ongoing rest of God and its completion in Jesus Christ? A verse in Hebrews hints this might be true: "There remains a Sabbath rest for the people of God, for whoever has entered God's rest has also rested from his works as God did from his" (4:9-10). So God's original command to rest could actually be a first glimpse of the greatness of God's purpose in Christ, calling us to a profound dependence on what we cannot complete or begin to imagine—a radical reliance on God's unutterable love and provision.

If this indeed is the call to the believer, why do we have such trouble with rest in our daily lives? One reason might be the time in which we live. This shuffling society, with distractions abounding, sometimes reminds me of an overloaded notebook with papers flying everywhere or an airport terminal full of important people rushing off on urgent errands. When everyone's rushing around—and urging *us* to rush around—settling down can be hard to do.

But I'm thinking there's a deeper reason. Could our resistance to rest be a piece of our very nature—our fallen nature, which cannot resist bucking God and rebelling? Upon looking back some thousands of years, we find evidence for that in the book of Exodus, where we read that even the Israelites in the wilderness needed to be reminded to slow down and take a rest. How could one possibly stay busy in the desert? After the goats had been milked, the sheep herded, and the tent tidied, what was there to do? And yet the people of Israel still resisted God's orders about the Sabbath.

God, you may remember, provided for His people in the wilderness by sending down a substance called manna every morning. And each family was to collect only what they could eat that day, with the exception of the sixth day. On the sixth day they were to gather two days' worth of manna so they could rest on the seventh.

It was a simple plan, really. Not too demanding. But not everyone liked it. In fact, many of the Israelites insisted on going out to gather on the seventh day.

## Sabbath Deprivation Disorder:
## Why God Commands Us to Rest

*On the seventh day some of the people went out to gather, but they found none. And the LORD said to Moses, "How long will you refuse to keep my commandments and my laws? See! The LORD has given you the Sabbath; therefore on the sixth day he gives you bread for two days. Remain each of you in his place; let no one go out of his place on the seventh day."*
*(Exodus 16:27-29)*

Were the Israelites worried about insufficient provision, concerned that God wouldn't do what He had said He would do? Or were they just plain greedy? I cannot answer the question with accuracy. I only know that many times I do the same kind of things they did. God says one thing, but I willfully do another. God says rest, and I do everything but.

Why? I believe it has to do with the fact that people have a fallen nature that rails against authority. In this case we rebel against a heavenly Father who has our best interest in mind. We think we know better than He does, and we want to do things our way. It's our time, remember? So we keep on going, driven by the clock, by the expectations of others, and by our own desires, racing along at someone else's speed other than God's. Our bodies ache, we thrash at night without sleep, and we live on the synthetic energy of caffeine and electric lighting. Like the Israelites—or like toddlers pushing every boundary—we're just not each ready to stay in our place.

But whether we like it or not, what we need is a break. And I'm talking about a real break—not a ten-minute Starbucks stop. Not a stolen Saturday night at the movies. Not even a two-hour nap on Sunday after church. I'm talking about a real change of pace. An entire day off from regular activities—on a regular, weekly basis. That's the kind of Sabbath the Bible prescribes—the kind that faithful people observed through the centuries—the kind of Sabbath that has all but disappeared in our hurried-up culture, even in many Christian circles.

You can probably come up with some reasons why this Sabbath rest has fallen out of favor. One reason is that we find it hard to resist the push of our twenty-four/seven society to do more, to hurry faster, to be more productive. Another is that legalism has sometimes turned God's gift of Sabbath into a joyless, rule-bound observance and soured entire generations on the Sabbath idea. Many Christians, too, have assumed that the practice of Sabbath is a matter of law and not grace and is therefore unnecessary under Christ. Then, of course, there's that nagging little problem of our rebellious human nature.

But the Bible makes it clear that all these reasons are really just excuses. We've already talked about how God, in Genesis, both modeled and commanded a regular rest from labor. And the New Testament reveals that Jesus did observe the Sabbath, though not in the legalistic way that the Pharisees would have liked. He even stated in Matthew 12:8 that "the Son of Man is lord of the Sabbath." Yet even as the CEO of the Sabbath, He kept this commandment in complete and honest obedience. Surely that should say something to us. But what? What shape should a Sabbath rest take in the real world?

### Take rest; a field that has rested gives a bountiful crop. (Ovid)

Until recently, to be honest, I never thought much about what breaking or keeping the Sabbath meant. To me, the practice seemed ancient, outdated, and very Hebrew. Then a funny thing happened. While directing a rehearsal for a Bible presentation, I listened to a recitation of the Ten Commandments by a group of eight-year-olds. And as I followed along, mouthing those familiar words, I found myself really hearing them for the first time. It occurred to me that while the Christian church as I knew it securely validated all the other commandments, I had never heard much about Sabbath rest. I don't remember hearing any sermons about it. I never really saw it practiced in the churches or the Christian universities I attended. So I had come to assume that Sabbath rest was simply an outdated notion. I figured my church attendance (or the guilt associated with not going to church) sufficed for Sabbath recognition.

If that's your experience, then the truth about Sabbath rest is going to be very eye-opening for you. It surprised me, and I have been a believer for thirty years.

The Sabbath, in the New Testament, is associated as a basic human *need*. Jesus stated this directly: "The Sabbath was made for man, not man for the Sabbath" (Mark 2:27). All the striving and rationalization in the world will not change those facts. You are human, and while you are able to work hard and efficiently for days, you are designed to perform best with regular time off.

And do you know the most bizarre part of this situation? You *want* a break. You are literally dying for it. Your emotions need refueling. Your mind needs some renewing. Your spirit needs some sweetness. And your poor body just needs a little relaxation—or maybe a little healthy exercise. It is the way humans are made.

I'll address in a later chapter some specifics about how you can go about incorporating true Sabbath rest into your family's life. But for now, are you ready to come to agree with God that a time should be set apart for rest, refueling, renewing, sweetness, and relaxation? Could the Sabbath become something positive in life? Instead of viewing it as one more thing you *have* to do, could you view it as a luxury you want to partake in—a sort of daylong spa treatment for your whole person? It's worth a try, and the benefits go far beyond a simple break from routine.

One of the most important elements of the Sabbath, in fact, is that it allows us to put things back in perspective. By honoring one day out of seven as a day to relax, to do something different, and to think about God, we are actually agreeing with God that our time is His. We concur that His ways are higher than our ways, that God is smarter and kinder than we are. And we reinforce that habit of thinking, thus building our capacity to trust Him. In a sense, Sabbath rest is a form of praise.

In addition, we usually discover lots of surprising little things— like the fact that we really were tired after all, and that the world will not stop if the laundry sits unfolded for a day, and best of all that God somehow allows for increased productivity despite the apparent loss of time.

Take a long look at the rising corporate star of Sabbath rest, Chick-Fil-A. In the rough-and-tumble world of corporate fast food, Chick-Fil-A has consistently refused to keep their doors open on Sunday. As a corporation, they've made the choice to observe a Sabbath rest for themselves and their employees, giving up a whole day in which they could generate business. And despite the loss of a day's worth of earnings each week, they have consistently found themselves at the number-one spot for customer service nationally.

I recently had the opportunity to visit Chick-Fil-A's national headquarters in Atlanta. We stopped by unexpectedly. We were greeted as though we had an appointment and were extended an invitation to eat in the employee cafeteria. And guess what? Those employees were not scurrying around at double speed, trying to make up for missing one day out of seven. I have to tell you, that group of people was the most hospitable, calm group of corporate Americans I have ever seen. They were living out the reality of God's Sabbath blessing.

What kind of blessings might you be missing by staying open twenty-four/seven? Is there any chance you'd be willing to try your hand at letting God do a little divine work on your schedule? Would you at least be willing to give it a try?

## Time Out

• Think of the last time you actually had a day off from your regular activities. How did you feel at the end of it? (If you can't remember a day off in the recent past, try to imagine what one would feel like.)

• Why do you think God made humans to need rest?

• Complete this statement, "I'd like to rest, but . . ."

• Upon completing the statement, compare that sentence to God's Word. How does it hold up?

• In what ways has your particular background—your childhood and adult experiences—prepared you to think about the Sabbath. What were you taught? What did you observe? How do you think that background has influenced your present-day attitude toward Sabbath rest?

• What specific commitments in your life make the idea of a complete day off seem impossible to you?

PART TWO

# The Truth About You:

### Making Peace with How God Made You . . . and Your Time

# The Time of Your Life

*God created time, and it's an amazing, awe-inspiring piece of work that deserves our respect and our careful attention. God designed His creation to be handled a certain way, and we prosper when we honor His design.*

*Interestingly enough, the same could be said about you and me.*

*Every single human being is created differently—and beautifully—by design. Each of us has our unique physical makeup, our particular history, our individual outlook, and our God-given personality. And each of us, in our own way, is an amazing, awe-inspiring piece of work that deserves our respect and careful attention, and we prosper when we honor His design and treat it the way God prescribed.*

*I love the way C. S. Lewis describes God's design in making humans as unique individuals:*

> I am considering not how, but why, He makes each soul unique. If He had no use for all these differences, I do not see why He should have created more souls than one. Be sure that the ins and outs of your individuality are no mystery to Him; and one day they will be no mystery to you. . . . Your soul has a curious shape because it is a hollow made to fit a particular swelling in the infinite contours of the Divine substance.[1]

*God as our Creator designed our "curious shape" and made us for "a particular swelling . . . of the Divine substance." Isn't that a lovely idea? The understanding that God not only loves each of us but designed us uniquely, with a special purpose in mind, is both humbling and flattering. And God as our Creator has the ultimate knowledge regarding our lives, our time, and our schedules. So it just makes sense that the better we understand ourselves and the way we're made, the better use we'll make of God's other creation—time.*

*This section is written to help you understand a little more of who you are, how your individual proclivities affect your use of time, and how you can best glorify God within the time He gave you. So plunge ahead, and let God help you discover more of the treasure He created in you.*

# 1rt:

## Real You

SILVER STAR
my mountain

I ... friend Liz laughingly t ... ...oaning to her on the pl.... about the fact that the new job I had taken required travel. And my feelings about travel were no secret to Liz, who had to coax me along to even attend our church's women's retreat some thirty minutes outside of town. I had many stipulations about who could be in our room, how many could be in our room, and so on. I carried along my pillow, shower shoes, and many other unnecessary items to make me feel more comfortable in that foreign land known as the women's retreat. I was mercilessly hounded for being "high maintenance," though Liz lovingly protected me from anything that might affect my actual stability when I was required to be away from home.

I confess (read: blame) that I have been severely infected by my homebody mother and sister. I credit both heredity and environment with my distaste for travel. But to be stigmatized as a flower so fragile was disturbing.

Oh, I loved thinking of the beauty of the orchid. Slender, exquisite, long-lasting—yes, I could live with that characterization. It was the connotation about not being flexible, about being a high-maintenance hothouse flower, that bothered me.

## The Time of Your Life

**My business is not to remake myself, but to make the very best of what God made. (Robert Browning)**

Why couldn't I be a daisy—happy and carefree? The kind of flower you take along to cheer someone. Or a rose—a constant classic that can be dressed up or dressed down. A favorite at weddings. Sought after by every sort of person. Oh, so popular.

But no. Honestly, I had to agree with Liz. She really knows me, and she was right: I am an orchid. Roots exposed, with my innermost feelings hanging out for the world to see. Destined to be happiest blooming in one place where the temperature and water schedule are just right, where I can avoid environmental extremes. Enjoying a dramatic presentation, yet secretly desiring simplicity. An artist at heart, producing a bloom and hanging on to the beauty of it as long as possible. Yes, I am an orchid. For better or for worse.

I hung up the phone and stared straight out the window. The sun was to the west, sending dappled light through the window. Within minutes I came to a decision.

I would accept the admirable side of my orchid-like self, all the things that come quite naturally to me. But I would not settle for orchid limitations when it was in my power to change. I would be the hardiest, most flexible orchid to grace the garden. I could be moved around, blooming all the while. I would pray about the areas where I needed to be open to change. My friends who knew me would no longer see fussy, hothouse behavior. Rather, they would marvel that an orchid could exhibit daisy-like behavior. I would let God's Spirit grow me into wellness in the areas where He saw fit.

Has it worked? I guess my friends and my traveling companions would have to tell you for sure. But I know that in subsequent years I have traveled all over the country with a relatively cheerful attitude. I'm still an orchid—always will be—and I'm learning to accept that fact, even cherish it. But I'm trying hard to be a portable, lower-maintenance one.

It's always a tricky thing, isn't it, to find a balance between accepting who we are and opening ourselves to being better? The temptation is always to fall to one extreme or another. One extreme is to give up all hope of improving, to allow our inevitable weaknesses to define us. And, at the other extreme, we may grow defensive, as I did at Liz's light-hearted comment. We may even end up denying or denigrating ourselves. As Nels F. S. Ferré puts it, "We hide from ourselves the parts which we do not like. We paint over such elements to make them seem strong and pretty; this we do with our eyes closed lest we should see ourselves as we are."[1]

**We make a terrible error when we think that to be human means to be perfect, some kind of unerring Christian model that cannot exist in reality. Only God is perfect. To be human is to be able to laugh, to cry, to live fully, to be aware of our lives as we are living them. (Madeleine L'Engle)**

Is there a way to avoid either extreme—to accept our limitations, yet still stretch out to a better self? I think there is. It's another form of balance. And it has a lot to do with trusting God.

The God who made you who you are.

The God who wants to make you even better.

These days I'm experiencing that kind of growth firsthand. I still dislike travel. I savor home, and I imagine I always will. I have lots of little home habits that help me feel balanced and secure. But now I have a job (and a calling) that requires me to stretch out of my comfort zone. I work with a ministry for girls and their mothers that sponsors events across the country, and I need to show up personally at many of them. All this opens me up to changes that sometimes create discomfort. But I want to go with God where He calls me. And He's made it fairly clear to me that this season of my life is about travel and staying in places that are unfamiliar.

I have learned to branch out, to accept that God will accompany me, to allow newness to take hold in my soul. I have moved to a new level of dependence on Him for my security. And I have found that the things He is planning for my life are actually fun, enjoyable. I'm being stretched, but I'm finding I'm far more flexible than I ever thought possible. God is teaching me, and I am His student.

Best of all, I have found that the more honest I am about myself, the more open I am to God's improvement, the more energy I have, and the less tired and busy I become. It's amazing. Learning to stretch has somehow seemed to stretch my available time as well. But I couldn't have begun that stretching process if I hadn't been willing to be real about myself first.

Psalm 86:11 states, "Teach me your way, O LORD, and I will walk in your truth; give me an undivided heart, that I may fear your name" (NIV).

I love that phrase: "*an undivided heart.*" It's the very opposite of conflicted, confused living.

An undivided heart is a heart that is united, one, true to who you are and who you are called to be, not denying the person God designed you to be. An undivided heart means being real about who you are. And that, in turn, allows you to operate at full capacity to complete your God-given tasks.

So who are you at the core of yourself—an orchid, a daisy, a rose, or some other flower altogether? Are you ready to accept that basic reality about yourself but remain open to ways that God may plan to change you?

If you have issues with understanding your created nature, you may be able to gain some insight by taking a personality test or a spiritual gifts survey. Or ask a wise and trusted friend to be brutally honest about how he or she sees you. It will be worth all the discomfort if you begin realizing that your constant struggle with the calendar may well represent a struggle with yourself. No matter what else you do, be sure to pray and ask God to reveal what you need to know about yourself. He has the answers, and He will honor your honesty.

Every January I make a list in my journal. On one side I list the things I dislike—all kinds of things. The year we had a puppy in the house, I actually included dog poop on my list. I laugh now at that. But caring for that puppy demanded extensive—and unwelcome—experience with dog poop. Another item on my dislike list that year was getting stalled out spiritually. And yet another was "bad barn days," which had to do with the fact that I was struggling with some of my horseback riding skills.

## An Undivided Heart:
## Accepting—and Improving—the Real You

**The longings of your heart are not incidental; they are critical messages. The desires of your heart are not to be ignored, they are to be consulted. As the wind turns the weather vane, so God uses your passions to turn your life. (Max Lucado)**

But dislikes aren't the only things that make my January lists. On the other side of my journal, I list the things I like. Thankfully, that same year the "like" list was much longer. I listed reading, writing, cool sunny weather, order, obedience, downtime, Liz and Sonja (two close friends), "whatever" hair (no excessive styling), being outside, fresh flowers. Lots of things.

My lists have proved to be quite humorous and enlightening over the years. But one thing I have noted is that some of the same issues keep surfacing. For example, I don't much like surprises. I can be competitive. I don't like to be so rushed that I don't have time for musing. I truly enjoy preparing meals for my family. I am enriched spiritually through art and nature and try to make time to enjoy them. These are the things I have come to know about myself. If I deny them, I tend to become uncomfortable, ill at ease. To be true to myself, I make time for the things that are important to me, that help me be fully myself. And when I do that, I find I am full enough to love the people in my life, who are my greatest priority.

I urge you, then, to open your eyes to the wonder of how God created you. There is truly a treasure waiting to be revealed. But also open your ears to His call on your life and be willing to branch out on His behalf and with His power. As you begin to look at yourself with your eyes wide open, you will see the truth of how lovingly you were designed.

And from there, you'll find it's easy to grow into who you were meant to be.

## Time Out

• Be honest: what parts of yourself do you tend to paint over so people won't see the real you—or wince when they notice it?

- Why do you think letting people see the real you can be so uncomfortable?
- Is it hard for you to imagine that God is smiling down on you, His creation? If so, why do you think this is difficult?
- What are the manifestations of living a divided life?
- List some of your qualities and behaviors that create conflict within you, causing time drain.
- In what ways is God currently asking you to stretch out and grow in some area of newness?
- What are the benefits of accepting who you really are? What are the drawbacks of refusing to see this?

# 9

# Take Care:

## Coming to Terms with Your Needs and Limitations

**If you picked up** this book in the first place, it's a good guess you're less than comfortable with life as you're living it right now. And if you've read this far, you probably sense that something needs to change. You may even have taken out your pencil and your Daytimer to begin making some changes.

*More Bible study. More time in prayer. Gotta have a Sabbath. Cut back on those coffee stops. Take a hike or two. Record likes and dislikes in my journal.*

That's all well and good.

But before you add another to-do or cross off another appointment or make another note, I urge you to stop and think about something more basic. Take a minute to consider what you need most in life. Realize that God desires balance for you, and that balance includes taking care of yourself physically, emotionally, and spiritually.

God wants you to take care of yourself because when you do, you are able to accomplish His plans for your life. And taking care of yourself involves knowing some basic facts about who you are in the first place. While I am not advocating excessive self-examination, I do believe that many of us wander through life recklessly because we have not taken the time to look at ourselves realistically. We fail to appreciate the uniqueness of God's design in us or the way our experiences have shaped us. More important, we fail to take into account either our personal limitations, our unique potential, or God's particular call on our lives. And taking these things into account is crucial. If you can grasp that God has a plan for your life, then it simply makes sense that He devised the plan with your distinct personality in mind.

"The God I know does not ask us to conform to some abstract norm for the ideal self," writes Parker Palmer. "God asks us only to honor our created nature, which means our limits as well as our potentials."[1] Honoring your created nature involves getting to know your true self, which in turn enables you to plan your time usage adequately and wisely. More important, it allows you to live at ease with yourself and with your schedule.

I'm not talking about a life of ease. I mean a kind of serenity, a comfortable acceptance of who God has made us to be. And to be honest, I can only think of a handful of people who routinely live with that kind of serenity.

My sister is one of them. She is at ease in her schedule and with herself. Her days are purposeful and full but never frantic. Even with a husband, four children, two dogs, a sizable house to care for, and loads of volunteer work at our church, she never moans about being either bored or too busy.

**When we truly care for ourselves, it becomes possible to care far more profoundly about other people. The more alert and sensitive we are to our own needs, the more loving and generous we can be toward others. (Eda LeShan)**

I wonder at that. Why aren't more people, Christians especially, like Linda? Doesn't it make sense that if we are with God, abiding in Him, we should be comfortable with ourselves and our life? With all the benefits of God's Spirit working in us, you would think we would routinely be the healthiest and most balanced people around. At peace with ourselves and at peace with others. Confidently playing the hand we were dealt, trusting in God to make up what we lack.

## Take Care:
## Coming to Terms with Your Needs and Limitations

But so many Christians I know (including me a lot of the time) are nothing of the sort. Instead, we're way too busy and way too tired. We struggle with stress-related illnesses—you know, migraines, TMJ, acid reflux, ulcers, insomnia, and the like. We battle workaholism, family dysfunction, control issues, depression, anger.

It's not that Christians as a group are any *worse* off than the general society. It's just that we should be so much *better* off. What is it that keeps us so uptight?

I'm sure that sin has something to do with it. So does failing to rely on God in a practical way and to draw on His spiritual provision for the energy we need. But could part of the problem also be that we fail to understand our created nature—to take a good look at who we really are and to honor the way God made us?

I can imagine what you are thinking: *I don't know about my created nature. All I know is that I'm living at my limit!*

But that's exactly the point. Honoring our created nature includes knowing what our limits are and adjusting our lives and schedules accordingly. Only when we do that can we truly take care of ourselves and begin to achieve the kind of ease God wants for us in our lives.

In the book of Exodus, Moses learned that lesson firsthand. It came at a time when he himself was living at the limit. He was surrounded by needy Israelites. Day after day he made himself available to assist the people with their problems and judge their disputes. And day after day the Israelites took advantage of Moses' availability. He was working from morning until evening, worn out by the thousands who depended on him.

Fortunately, Moses' father-in-law, Jethro, looked a very tired Moses straight in the face and challenged him to take a look at himself and his limitations. He told him flat-out, "What you are doing is not good. You and the people with you will certainly wear yourselves out, for the thing is too heavy for you. You are not able to do it alone" (Exodus 18:17-18).

Moses listened to his father-in-law and took his advice. He appointed a number of subordinate leaders to take care of the smaller issues and settle minor disputes. Then he was free to use his time and energy for his main priorities—leading his people and representing them before God. What a great example for us of coming to terms with what we can't do and making wise choices in the light of those limitations.

The truth is that understanding our limitations is one of the main ways we can learn about our God-created selves. What are these limitations? They include those common to all humans (we all need sleep) and those unique to us (I personally need at least eight hours of sleep a night). They may be physical in nature (short people can only reach so high) or related to personality (very introverted people tire out quickly in crowds). They can also be circumstantial or related to a particular season in life (moms with young children have certain constrictions on their time).

But whatever your limitations are (and we all have them), be aware that God earnestly desires balance and abundance for you. Accepting them is part of knowing the truth about who you are, not being blinded by misconceptions about self or a stubborn refusal to accept what we can or cannot do. In a word, it involves understanding who you are and how much, with God's help, you can handle.

If, as in the case of Moses, you are already at your limit, then you might well be wise to let the circumstances speak—and not only the circumstances, but those who care about you. If you listen carefully, you may well hear a Jethro in your life telling you that you have taken on more than you are designed to handle. Maybe it is your spouse, your employer, your friends, maybe even your in-laws.

But let's face it—honoring our limitations isn't easy. It takes courage to face the truth that we just can't do everything we want to do—not to mention other people's opinions about what we should or shouldn't be doing. That kind of courage is part of the price we pay for learning to be at ease with life. But the results are definitely worth the price. In the long run it's far easier—and more joyful—to take care of ourselves by being realistic about who we are, what we are being called to do, and what we need in order to fulfill our calling.

I love the passages in the New Testament when Jesus encounters people who need healing. One of my favorites is when Jesus meets the blind beggar in Luke 18:35-43. Upon meeting the man, the Son of God says, "What do you want me to do for you?" The beggar replies, "Lord, let me recover my sight." To which Jesus says, "Recover your sight; your faith has made you well."

## Take Care:
## Coming to Terms with Your Needs and Limitations

**The Lord still calls us to follow Him beside still waters on a regular basis so He can restore us. But He never forces us to do what is good for us. When He calls, we have to follow. (Alice Gray and Steve Stephenson)**

Think for a moment about that dialogue. Jesus asked an obviously blind man what He wanted—it's ludicrous, isn't it?

Or is it? Perhaps not.

You see, I believe God is as interested in our self-awareness as He is in our healing. He wants us to recognize and acknowledge both who we are and what we need from Him. I also think He wants us to desire to see things with spiritual eyes. And that too was part of what Jesus was saying to the blind beggar. By asking him what he wanted, Jesus was helping the man focus on his deepest need: Christ Himself.

Do you want to see the truth about yourself? Do you want to know what God desires to speak into your life? Do you really want to stop living at the limit (or beyond)? Or is your real desire, in your heart of hearts, to catch your breath so you can run harder?

If you really desire to see yourself as God made you, to live at ease with yourself and your life, then God will honor that desire. He will supply whatever energy and wisdom you need to live according to your created nature and to do whatever He calls you to do.

God is always communicating to you through the people in your life, through your circumstances, through the quiet voice of His Spirit, and He is waiting on you with the same question: "What do you want me to do for you?" Do you want to live a balanced life? Do you want to see yourself as you are made to succeed in God's plan?

And don't forget that coming to terms with your created nature involves more than just accepting your limits. It also means paying attention to your gifts and your God-created potentials. After all, God made you as far more than a package of limitations. He has gifted you uniquely with talents, experiences, and capabilities that are needed in this world. You honor that creation when you do whatever you can to discover what these are and to use them in God's service. Parker Palmer puts it this way:

If we are to live our lives fully and well, we must learn to embrace the opposites, to live in a creative tension between our limits and our potentials. We must honor our limitations in ways that do not distort our nature, and we must trust and use our gifts in way that fulfill the potentials God gave us.[2]

Would you be willing to ask God to reveal both your limits and potentials? If you are in earnest about understanding yourself in light of His design and purpose, then you must know that He will meet you with honest—and loving—answers.

## Time Out

• In what ways do you routinely take care of yourself? Consider the physical (diet, nutrition, basic health habits), the emotional, and the spiritual.

• Is there an area where you know you are failing to take proper care of the you whom God created? What are some of the reasons for this neglect?

• Identify at least one person in your life who routinely is at ease with his or her life schedule. What qualities create the healthy balance in that person's life?

• Who is your Jethro, and what has he or she told you to do to relieve your stress?

• List at least three strategies for getting help with your load like Moses did. (Be creative!)

• Describe your positives and your potentials both physically (what you can achieve with your body) and where your personality is concerned. Do this prayerfully and generously.

• Ask a trusted friend to lunch, and allow her to help you identify any blind spots concerning your life and your schedule.

# 10

# The Tempo of Truth:

## Living at Your Built-in Speed

**I am an early riser.** I get up every morning by at least 5:20. I have such passion about the beauty of the dawn that I wouldn't dream of wasting its serenity by sleeping in, regardless of the previous day's load.

If you do the math, you can probably guess I am not a night owl. Darkness says to me, "Sleep," and I willingly obey. There is nothing more pleasing to me than taking a warm shower, slathering on scented lotion, and folding myself into my favorite inanimate object: my bed. I sing as I climb in with the glee of a child with a double-decker ice cream cone. I am absolutely wiped out after 9 in the evening. Nothing is really very funny to me after that hour. In fact, I have a strongly held belief that nothing serious should be discussed after then—and that nothing of much value goes on after that time.

The trouble is, my son feels the same way about anything that happens before 7 in the morning. His energy peaks about the time I become radioactive at night. But if I would try to wake him at 7 (which is midmorning for me) to discuss anything of any value, I would be wasting my time. When he was still in high school, I was lucky to get a pause at the door for a kiss on the cheek from him as he left the house. Some days I wasn't even sure he was awake.

My love of morning is lost on my son, and he teases me about my bedtime. Our body clocks are completely out of sync. But we have come to respect the fact that we are very different and that there is no use trying to change each other.

It's not just a matter of body clock either. Sometimes I think the two of us move at completely different speeds.

The night after my son graduated from high school, there was an all-night party at a local pizza/arcade establishment. My sister (who also had a graduate) and I agreed to chaperone the 11-at-night-to-1-in-the-morning slot. When we arrived at the restaurant, the kids scattered through the place like hungry mice—grabbing hot pizza, buzzing down sodas, and playing all the blaringly loud arcade games. After a casual stroll through the arcade area, I settled in with the other parent chaperones, sitting on the benches in the large hallway.

I needed to sit down. I needed to be away from the loudness in the arcade room. But what I *really* needed was some sleep.

I didn't get it—at least not much. After two hours and some excessive rounds of card playing, my chaperoning commitment came to an end, but by that time I had gotten carried away with the fun and stayed longer than I expected. By the time I finally got home and my head hit the pillow, it was 3:30 in the morning.

I guess I don't need to tell you that I woke up the next morning feeling as sick as I've ever been. It took me a full forty-eight hours to get over the sleep I had lost that night. Meanwhile, my son stayed up all night and then, some forty-eight hours later, was off to the next adventure—a week of church camp for more fun, more greasy food, and more late nights.

**Being balanced is not so much a matter of staying in perfect equilibrium as it is a matter of finding the right rhythm for our lives. (Joanna Weaver)**

What did I learn from that experience? That physically speaking, forty-something morning people cannot keep up with eighteen-year-old night owls. As close as I feel to eighteen in my mind (didn't I just graduate yesterday?), the truth is that I am a middle-aged woman. (I am cringing here.) I am likely halfway through my life, and I have the body and the energy level to prove it. As easy as it is to long for those good old days when I could really eat anything I wanted and physically accomplish almost anything I wanted, I am no longer the person I was back then. I cannot stay up half the night without paying the price, any more than I can wolf down loads of pizza without paying the price.

Ah, the tempo of truth. Time exacts its toll on what we can do with our time.

A casual look at classical music will tell us a little more about how different tempos affect our lives. As you may know, most printed music contains notes from the composer—usually in Italian—explaining how the piece is to be played. Some of these notes concern loudness or softness, but many are about speed, or tempo. Some of the common classical music tempo notations are *adagio*, *moderato*, and *presto*. *Adagio* means slow. *Moderato* means moderate. *Presto* means fast. In any given piece, a variety of tempos creates a richness and freshness for musicians and listeners alike.

Our lives are much like music in that respect. Each person we know moves through life at a slightly different speed—it's part of our personalities, the way God made us. Some, by nature, live an *adagio* life, slow and stately, unwilling to be pushed. Some of us are *presto* people—fast-moving and fast-talking, wired to race through our days. And even those of us in the middle, the *moderatos*, vary in our God-directed speed of moving through life.

We differ too, as my son and I differ, in the tempo of our days, slowing at certain hours, speeding up at others. And each season of life brings its own new tempos as well. No matter what our natural tendency, we all go through slower times and faster times, and we all tend to slow down as we age.

*Adagio, moderato, presto*—when we follow the specific tempos God has composed for each of us, our lives feel rich and fresh and interesting. But what happens when we pull against the appropriate tempo, trying to speed things up or slow them down or to play everything the same speed? The result can be jarring or dull or frantic, but it's certainly not beautiful music.

When I awoke the morning after the graduation ceremony and

party, I felt a rush of different emotions. One was awe that I was the mother of a high-school graduate. One was surprise that I felt so sick from the sleep deprivation. (It wasn't that long ago that I was pulling an all-nighter studying for college finals, was it?) I also—and this one surprised me—felt a certain sadness in remembering how it felt to live at *presto*, with the utter exuberance of youth. But that tempo is gone, and another, much more complex one has replaced it. So I now enjoy the *presto* in my son's composition while I listen to the more sedate *moderato* in my own.

As we age, we slow down; that's the way God made life work. As much as I might like to recapture the time known as youth, that speed is gone in my life. Recapturing it would be as silly and inappropriate as dressing up this forty-year-old body in the clothing of a sixteen-year-old.

No one speed in life is inherently good or bad. But the speed of life at any given point should be determined by the composer's intent. It would be entirely inappropriate to hear a piece composed and marked *adagio* to be played *presto*. And the reverse is true. We need to strive toward moving at the pace we are set to, not the pace around us.

But that raises a problem in our hurry-up culture. Someone set the metronome on *presto*, so we all speed along with no regard to how God designed us or what is appropriate for our season. And the result is not only a lot of stress, but an emptier, less interesting life.

No matter what our culture tells us, *adagio* does not mean valueless. There is no need to feel dismayed at a somewhat slower tempo. While the world yells "Hurry," God does not. All He wants is for us to pay attention to the nature He gave us and the needs of our particular season—to move according to the tempo He prescribes.

Does this mean we should *never* vary our comfortable tempo to respond to the needs of others? Of course not. God didn't put us here on earth just to attend to our own comfort. And there are certainly times when we might want to adjust our personal tempo in the interest of harmony. A naturally fast talker might need to hold back a little to keep from interrupting a slower-talking friend. Or an *adagio* type who prefers to work at a slow and deliberate pace might choose to speed things up at times to keep a *presto* colleague from overheating (though a better long-run choice would be to divide the work to take advantage of the different work styles.) A skipping child can certainly be taught to walk slowly with her aged relatives. And I did, after all, agree to chaperone my son's graduation party and lived to tell about it!

**Jesus does not speak about a change of activities, a change in contacts, or even a change of pace. He speaks about a change of heart. (Henri J. M. Nouwen)**

But all these are temporary and conscious adjustments made deliberately to accommodate others. It's one thing to show honor and respect for the tempos of others and quite another to try to live our lives at a speed that's not right for us.

In order to succeed at spending our time wisely, we must begin to see who we really are as well as where we are in life and to accept that God designed us all differently, with varying tempos. Each of us must look realistically at the way we are made and our natural tendencies—characteristics that affect our feelings about how we spend time. The comparison games we play, looking at others' ability to get things done or to move at a faster pace, only set us up to feel dissatisfied with our own tempo or to push others inappropriately to live at our speed instead of theirs.

I urge you: do whatever is necessary to uncover your natural self—your God-created self, not the schedule-driven woman who jump-starts herself with caffeine to keep pace, or the woman on the hunt for her past, desiring the speed of youth. Become aware of when you need rest, as I did after the late-night party, or when you need to just dive in and take care of a problem quickly. Accept the tempo that's appropriate for your personality and your stage in life.

Psalm 139:1-3 tells us, "O LORD, you have searched me and known me! You know when I sit down and when I rise up; you discern my thoughts from afar. You search out my path and my lying down and are acquainted with all my ways."

God designed you uniquely and ordained you for the very life you are leading. An honest look at the real you will open your life for authentic living. The kind of living that requires some deep thinking about God and the ability to see yourself as you really are. Your little tendencies are no surprise to God. He actually loves those things about you.

At a recent speaking engagement, I spoke about each person's being uniquely made by God. Afterward a beautiful young woman named Tina confessed to me, ashamedly, that she had often been called a "turtle" because she moved so slowly. As you know, *slow* in our culture is considered the near equivalent of stupid. But before Tina could blink, her friend Karen, who was standing nearby, blurted out, "You're not a turtle; you're a panda. You are warm and lovable and wonderful to be around." Tina's eyes filled with tears. She had needed an affirmation, and Karen gave it to her.

May I affirm you? You are created by God—wonderfully made, an awesome work. You are completely known by God. You delight Him. He is thinking about you right now. His hand of blessing is on your head, and there is nothing about you that surprises Him. He knows what you are going to say before you say it. He also knows about your time needs. He understands your stress. He sees your difficulty in managing all that is set before you. He knows how to help you accomplish what you are here for, and He is ready to help.

If that's hard for you to believe, I suggest spending some time with the first eighteen verses of Psalm 139. I am deeply moved by this section of Scripture, in which God affirms us so tremendously. He confirms that He holds the knowledge of our time—our days—in His hands.

Isn't that incredible? He knows the perfect speed for this season in your life—and He wants you to know it too.

The Lord God has not set us up to fail. He directs us through our basic tendencies and our daily choices, leading us gently to the place where we can be real with who we are and also, in a completely practical way, meet the demands of our days. When we allow Him to direct our lives, we will automatically move at the right pace.

Sometimes faster.

Sometimes slower.

Always beautiful to His ears.

## Time Out

• What recent experiences have made you aware of the tempo of truth?

• Think of a time when you have shared close quarters with someone who lived at a different tempo. What feelings or tensions did you encounter? How did you adjust to one another?

• If you are moving at a pace that is out of sync with God's design for your life, whether too fast or too slow, how might the music of your life sound to others?

• In your social circle, what would you say is driving the tempo of life?

• If you are a parent, what drives the tempo of your child's/children's social circle(s)? How does that affect your life speed?

• If you had an opportunity to change your tempo in order to maximize your life, would you slow down or speed up? Why?

# 11

# The Proverbial Plate:

## Living at Your Best Capacity

**The actual demands of** our days can send even our real selves running. We can know who God designed us to be and try in earnest to face our real needs honestly . . . and still get in a ton of trouble.

You see, I'm the lady at the grocery store who thinks she'll run in at 5 in the afternoon and just pick up ten items—only ten items because that way I can get through the "Ten Items or Less" checkout line. I pick up the little red-handled basket, throw it over my arm, and commence with shopping. "Ten items or less," I mutter to myself.

I head to the back of the store to get the sour cream, and on the way there I notice the Doritos. *Those Doritos will make Emily so happy.* I pick them up.

On to the sour cream, and then I pick up the frozen spinach. As I am leaving the frozen-food section, I remember that Sara wanted taquitos. *She needs them for an after-school snack*, I reason to myself.

*Oh yes*, I tell myself, *Will is out of his favorite cereal.* I head toward the cereal aisle, but not without passing the crackers, the ones Emily asked me to get. I pick up both items.

My basket is getting full, but I still have fewer than ten items. Good. I'm still in line for the quick check. Deli meat is next. And bananas. (I love this item because no matter how many bananas I pick up, they are only counted as one at the checkout.)

## The Time of Your Life

My arm is starting to hurt because the little basket is bulging with groceries. I balance it against my hip and hold the overflow with my free hand as I maneuver through the crowded store. I am now at ten items. The shopping must stop. I direct my eyes toward the checkout lanes. *No more*, I tell myself. However, as I am inching toward the front of the store, walking down the paper goods aisle, I spy the trash-can liners. *We're out of liners*, I mentally utter in desperation. That's eleven, and I'm legally over my limit.

With my original goal gone, I start looking around for a shopping cart. I might as well get everything I need now. I'll have to use the regular checkout lane with all the other 5 o'clock shoppers.

It's a daily picture of overloading the proverbial plate.

I'm talking about the combination of tasks and commitments that make up your daily schedule. I'm also talking about the size of your plate—your internal capacity to cope with whatever happens to you in life. We all have varying abilities to handle specific types of loads, whether they are physical, emotional, mental, or spiritual. We get that capacity from God; it's part of the way we're made. But many of us run through life without a thought for what our plate size is.

**When you put it all together—your natural pace and your capacity—what do you have? Superman? Wonder Woman? Probably not, because you are only human. Does that disappoint you? It should be a relief. After all, your body and your friends have known it all along. When you are true to yourself, you follow your natural bent and encourage others to follow theirs. You don't compare yourself to others or impose your preferences on anyone. You were not made in a mold, so you shouldn't force yourself or others to conform to one. (Charles Bradshaw and Dave Gilbert)**

Just think of the people you know. If you just look at just your immediate family, you can probably start to see what I mean.

Some people seem to be born with extra-large plates. These are the people who can take on the world and never be stressed out. They have a natural ability to handle lots of things at the same time. These people tend to be self-starters. They are always looking for the next adventure, the next job, and the endless rush of change—grabbing more for their plates and invigorated by the process of piling more and more on.

Other people, however, seem to have smaller plates. They are happier doing one thing at a time. They resist change, abhor multitasking, and thrive on what is simple and predictable.

It's important to note that the size of a person's plate has little to do with what they can accomplish in life. A small-plate person, after all, is perfectly capable of finishing one set of tasks and going back for more. But no matter the size of the plate, loading too much on it causes stress and can even lead to disaster—missed appointments, broken promises, emotional turmoil, guilt.

So it helps to know the size of our plate and to move through the buffet line accordingly. With wisdom and experience we can start to see who we really are and what feels comfortable to us. In addition, with God's help we can listen carefully to Him and move things on and off our proverbial plates in a way that reduces stress and maximizes our use of time.

Yes, I know, that's easier said than done, especially in our overloaded culture.

Undoubtedly, many days you set out determined to consider your plate size and not overload your life with unnecessary activities and commitments. But maybe you're like me at the grocery store and just can't help going past your original limit. Something looks fun or one of the kids really wants to do something or somebody asks you for a big favor . . . and your plate starts to fill up. A few more lessons and promises, and the plate is already overfull. But despite our extreme busyness, we keep adding items to our plates without thinking of the consequences.

In an op-ed piece entitled "Our Time-Crunch Disorder," Ellen Goodman ponders our inability to adequately count the cost of adding further commitments to an already busy schedule.

# The Time of Your Life

I wonder how many people suffer from timing disorders. How many make commitments *now* with the absolute and inaccurate certainty that we will have more time *then*. Do we look into the future and see an image as distorted as the anorexic who looks into the mirror?

This year, a pair of marketing professors from North Carolina published research about time and timing. The students surveyed said repeatedly they would have more free time on the same day of the next week or the next month than they had today. If you asked these students to add a commitment today, they would answer no. But ask them to do it in the future and they were more likely to say yes.

These students were not just a bunch of cockeyed optimists. The same people had a much more realistic view of their budgets. They were less likely to commit to spending more money in the future than in the present.

But in this sense, time was not money. It was more malleable. When thinking about their spare time, they experienced what researchers called "irrational exuberance." Even those on overload today would take on a fresh load in the future.[1]

It's hard for me to imagine that most of the overloaded people I know are suffering from "irrational exuberance," but I agree with the author of that article that a lot of us seriously miscalculate our time. We irrationally assume that we'll awake one month from now and will have finished with our current responsibilities and so will be able to take on new and weightier loads. So we commit today to tomorrow's debt by loading up more and more on today's plate. And though we are on over-load today, we continue to load up for the future.

To compound the problem, we don't always have a say in what gets loaded on our plate and when. Unexpected developments—a new baby, a job loss, an illness, even a dog that follows you home—can add just enough to our plates to overload them. I know that I often fail to take life's surprises into account. I don't leave room in my schedule for emergencies. Instead I attempt to manage whatever comes along, confused as to why I am having trouble coping.

I was recently talking with a friend who had the same problem. This poor woman had just lost her husband to cancer. She was tired, stressed, and exasperated over her inability to "get it all done." What seemed obvious to me, though not to her, was the fact that she'd previously had two plates—her husband's and hers—for handling family responsibilities. Now she only had one plate, but she still had two platefuls of responsibilities.

Sometimes life does that. There are times in life when we don't choose our situations—they choose us. That's another reason to be alert for the overwhelming feeling of having too much to do and too little time to do it. When the alarm sounds in your life, prepare yourself for some changes in your calendar. You might need to unload something from your plate.

The more predictable seasons of life can also affect your plate size—your ability to handle what commitments you can take on. Adolescence, young motherhood, empty nests, menopause, retirement—such events involve emotional adjustments and physical changes that can reduce the number of additional commitments we can carry in our schedules. Seasons are a part of life, and though we give thought to them, often they still manage to take us by surprise.

**Live in each season as it passes; breathe the air, drink the drink, taste the fruit. . . . And be thankful. (Henry David Thoreau)**

Where are you? How much is required of you? Are the expectations reasonable, and can you handle them? Are you ready and willing to be honest with yourself, to decide what activities in your life are most important and perhaps knock some others off your plate because of unexpected circumstances or the season of life where you find yourself?

Recently I had a conversation with a woman whom God is in the process of healing regarding some things that happened in her childhood. Normally she is a high-energy, self-motivated person with a positive, breezy personality and a willingness to take on the world. But this season of healing process, with its recognition of loss, has slowed her way down. She is outside of her "regular" self and just can't handle as much as she normally could. The season will pass, of course, and she will regain the ability to load up her plate with its usual-sized portions.

# The Time of Your Life

But for now she can't handle the regular load. She absolutely feels the need to calm her life down. She likens herself to a fussy, tired toddler screaming her head off on the inside.

She mused out loud, "Am I going crazy?"

"No," I answered. "But if you were my child, I would place you on house arrest and allow you only to participate in the essentials."

She looked at me blankly, and then her face crushed into tears. "What are the essentials?"

When we steadfastly refuse to take such matters as surprises and seasons into account, we set ourselves up for disaster. Things start sliding off the plate simply because there is literally no more room. We forget appointments, show up late for meetings, renege on our promises. We can't keep up with all the regular demands, and we feel crazy watching our customary schedule fly out the door. How much better it would be to keep an eye on our plates, making adjustments as needed to live more balanced lives.

The familiar words of Ecclesiastes 3:1-8 remind us that we were never intended to live with the same load, year after year:

> For everything there is a season, and a time for every matter under heaven:
> a time to be born, and a time to die;
> a time to plant, and a time to pluck up what is planted;
> a time to kill, and a time to heal;
> a time to break down, and a time to build up;
> a time to weep, and a time to laugh;
> a time to mourn, and a time to dance;
> a time to cast away stones, and a time to gather stones together;
> a time to embrace, and a time to refrain from embracing;
> a time to seek, and a time to lose;
> a time to keep, and a time to cast away;
> a time to tear, and a time to sew;
> a time to keep silence, and a time to speak;
> a time to love, and a time to hate;
> a time for war, and a time for peace.

For each season, this passage assures us, different behaviors are appropriate. We're *supposed* to change our activities as our lives change. But realistically, do we treat the seasons in our life with such distinction?

A woman I know lost her mother suddenly and unexpectedly—a drastic change in her life. Just like a tsunami, her bereavement swept over her with no apparent warning and left only raw devastation in its wake. And yet my friend kept pushing on, determined to keep up with her regular schedule, looking for comfort in her familiar routine—for a while, that is. But she could only go so far before the tremendous pain in her life caused her to slow down. Finally she began to recognize she just couldn't do as much.

But it took an emotional tidal wave to get her to unload her plate.

Why is it that some of us are so stubborn about recognizing when our plates are overloaded? Is it discomfort or embarrassment? Is it pride? What are we saying as we forge ahead, overloaded plate held high, refusing to recognize that our lives have changed and we need to change too?

All too often, I believe, our proverbial plates are piled so high that we don't even have time to stop and consider what we're doing; we're too frantic to reason things through. But could it also be that in some cases we're rebelling against God's ordained plan for our lives? Or perhaps, like my friend, we don't like the particular season we're in or the direction our lives have taken, and we respond by pretending nothing has changed.

A baby is born, and we rush back to work. There is a death, and we resume our normal schedule as quickly as possible. In some people's cases, you would never even know their lives have changed. With a blink, the plate is nauseatingly full, yet we keep scooping the oozing contents back on top.

We don't know full.

We don't know stop.

We simply don't know.

So we simply push on until it all crashes to the floor.

Because the truth is, we can't overload our plates forever. Large plate or small plate, we all have a finite capacity—that's just part of being human. We can only pile our plates so high before something happens. We drop the ball at work. Or we get distracted and cause a fender bender. Or the doctor gives us bad news about our blood pressure.

How much wiser we would be to keep an eye on our plates as we move through the buffet line of life, choosing carefully what we add, putting back items as necessary (do this in life, not in a real buffet line!), and staying in constant touch with our heavenly Father, relying on Him to help us do this according to His plan.

I have a little "thorn . . . in [my] flesh" (see 2 Corinthians 12:7) that actually helps me do this. It keeps me honest about my real self, my proverbial plate, and my schedule. It is my sensitive stomach. I cannot move very far outside of God's limit for me and my schedule without my stomach's clenching into spasms. If I go too overboard, my stomach cramps make my whole person take notice.

I used to hate that about myself, despising the weakness. Now I view my sensitivity as God's reminder to me that I have pushed myself too far. On occasion when I must keep functioning I will calm it with the little green pill my doctor gave me. But most of the time I try to listen to the groaning with a spiritual ear, knowing there a great possibility that I need more rest, some life pacing, and some God direction. It just makes sense.

Maybe you, like me, need to make some sense of your real self, your proverbial plate, your season of life, and the Holy Spirit's whispering. You may not have a sensitive stomach to help you along, but your body and your emotions and your times with God will give you signals about how much you can take. But it's up to you to learn to listen for those signals and to heed them.

Ecclesiastes 8:5 tells us, "The wise heart will know the proper time and the just way." That's especially true when it comes to understanding your capacity at any specific time of your life and making choices accordingly.

God will direct your open heart. Pray honestly for His answers as you seek His will for your life. If God were to sit down with you and your list of things to do, would you be willing to look Him in the face? What would He say to you? Would He recommend house arrest or point out ways that you have let your plate become overloaded?

God is not interested in making you feel stupid. Nor does He want you to be sick. He desires balance and awareness. He manages the time and the seasons, and He is willing to manage you too.

You can trust Him, even with your proverbial plate.

## Time Out

• What experiences/situations in a typical week tend to overfill your proverbial plate?

• How might you create a buffer in your daily or weekly schedule to accommodate those experiences or situations?

• Look back at a time when you experienced a surprising or sudden change of season in your life. What feelings surfaced during that time?

• Ecclesiastes 3:1-8 speaks of many seasons in life. How might you complete this sentence: "Right now is a time to . . ."?

# PART THREE
# Time Traps:

## Avoiding Unhealthy Schedule Choices

# The Time of Your Life

*I have a friend who was pulled over recently for speeding. She had breezed down a hill in an area with wide lanes and low traffic . . . right past a police car nestled by some live oak trees. It was a classic speed trap.*

*"I couldn't have been going that fast!" my friend told the officer. She was so sure she hadn't been speeding that she asked to see her recorded speed on the radar gun. She was indignant, quite sure she had not broken any speeding laws. But her posted speed was right there, documented on his radar. She'd fallen right into the trap, and she got a ticket as a result.*

*Time traps are like that in life. We are moving along, following the schedule of our life, and somehow we fall right into a time trap. We get fooled into making bad choices about our schedules and commitments. Sometimes we even fool our- selves. Then we feel indignant and wonder where all our time went or why we're being ticketed with relational problems, health concerns, or emotional distress.*

*These time traps we fall into cause us to lose time. We squander our energy because we weren't aware of or disregarded the set limit. We need to look honestly at what is going on with these time traps because then we can become aware and avoid them.*

*There are all kinds of time traps out there. And every one of those traps tells us something about our internal motivations because time traps always involve unwise, unhealthy choices. Almost all involve predictable foibles of human nature; they are traps because they're so easy to fall into. And it is only in recognizing them, noting what they are and where they are, that we can avoid them.*

*In her inspiring little book* Let Us Have Faith *Helen Keller addressed the truth about all the little choices in each day. "We betray ourselves into smallness," she wrote, "when we think the little choices of each day are trivial."[1] All the little choices of our day matter. And it is only by examining them and looking into the unhealthy choices that you can get to the heart issues and avoid those draining time traps.*

*Let God show you how to navigate through all those matters (for He is not a policeman to avoid) and you will find that as you are freed with new knowledge about your time traps, you will be making the very most of your time—the way God intended.*

# 12

# Greenspanning:

## The Trap of Inappropriate Panic

**As I write these chapters,** a man named Alan Greenspan holds the position of Chairman of the Board of Governors of the Federal Reserve System. He's held that position since 1987. And during his years as chairman, this remarkable man has wielded uncanny influence on our country's finances.

Dr. Greenspan's job is to warily watch the national economy and maintain essential financial equilibrium. He sets interest rates. He decides whether or not to print more currency. He identifies trends of inflation and deflation and prescribes adjustments to control these trends. You could think of him as the nation's banker, holding our collective currency in his hands.

It's a big job, and Alan Greenspan is a powerful man. But to me the most interesting thing about him is how people react to his pronouncements. When Alan Greenspan speaks, he sets a flurry of activity into motion. Just a few words from this man can trigger unbelievable stock activity, a frenzy of home buying and selling, even changes in our national habits of spending and saving. His reports have the power to hit a panic button, setting off financial alarms that create cumulative havoc.

And I can do that too, I've found. Not financially. Not nationwide.

But I am definitely the Alan Greenspan of our family. As wife and mother, I have the capacity to push the panic button and create cumulative havoc.

Just the other night, for example, I hit the alarm. My teenaged son called in and asked if he and a load of his friends could come over in ten minutes and play cards.

"Sure," I replied with ease. Then I hung up the phone, looked around at the abundant little messes around me . . . and reached for that panic button.

"Sara, take your backpack and homework to your room."

"Emily, put the dishes in the dishwasher."

And just as my husband walked in through the garage with his hands completely full, I issued a command to him too: "Please close the garage door; it's a wreck in there. Some kids are coming over, and I don't want them traipsing through the garage."

During those next ten minutes, I went scurrying about like a madwoman on a mission, barking orders as I went, and getting results. Clean laundry was carried to appropriate rooms. Piles of mail were tucked in drawers. Sofa pillows were fluffed. A throw blanket was folded. A dirty bath towel was taken to the hamper. A hand towel was replaced. A trash can was emptied.

## You cannot antagonize and influence at the same time. (John Knox)

The air in our house seemed thick with the bleating of an air raid. "Hurry! Hurry! Hurry!" I was in full panic mode, greenspanning, stirring up the whole household. The problem was, I was doing it over something of very little consequence. While there are occasions for quick emergency action (for example, when blood and doctors are involved), that was certainly not one of them. I set off the alarm to get the house clean for a bunch of teenagers when all they really needed was cards, popcorn, and a bowl full of M&Ms.

Do you ever find yourself doing that—calling out for help with a *big* problem that is actually not a big problem at all? I think many of us do that from time to time. In the process we not only waste our time—

we also create a lot of unnecessary stress for ourselves and those who share our lives.

I'll never forget the day I got a phone call from a frantic friend of mine. She sounded irate and baffled. "I am so stressed out! The maid arrived at the bus stop late, and I had to *wait* for her, then take her *all the way back* to the house. Then I had to *go all the way to the school* (read: private Christian school—*cha-ching!*) to pick up the kids because we have to get packed because we're *desperately* trying to get ready to go skiing for spring break! This is so *irritating!* I feel so exhausted. I just don't have enough *time!*"

Hmmm, let's analyze this. Mom is stressed because she had to pick up her housekeeper to clean her large house. She is irritated because she had to retrieve children from a cozy, safe Christian school. She is exhausted because she is going on a fun family ski trip. Hmmm.

With each of my friend's breathless complaints, I remember thinking, *This is really not that big of a problem. She is living life like a tornado whirled up in a perceived panic cycle.* But of course that was easy for me to see. It was *her* panic, not mine!

What about you? Do you save your hurrying and scurrying for real emergencies? Or do you live the hysterics of a tornado lifestyle, driven on by a skewed perspective and using your greenspanning powers to throw your whole household into a panic?

That skewed, hurried perspective is everywhere you look. Just take a look at the drivers on your local highway. The majority of motorists in my part of the world drive as though they are on the way to the emergency room or speeding by on some mission of great importance. More likely, they're just on their way to work and running a little behind. But they dart ahead at signals, weave in and out of lanes, tailgate the drivers ahead of them, and honk out their frustrations, just as if they were in a real emergency.

I honestly hate that kind of behavior. I truly believe there are enough real emergencies in life that we don't have to create our own. And my sincere desire as a wife and mother is a balanced, peaceful life for my family. I don't want to make too much out of the little stuff. I don't want my children (and husband) to feel like they are living a pressure-packed life. I don't want to greenspan when it's not appropriate.

But as much as I despise my own premature punches on the panic button, I seem to still hit it too frequently. How can you and I get to the place where we don't set off unnecessary alarms?

There is a biblical story that has helped me discern when it is appropriate to hurry and when it isn't. In 1 Samuel 25 we read about a woman named Abigail who panicked appropriately and was rewarded for it. The story goes something like this.

David and his warriors were in the wilderness and had been watching over and protecting the shepherds of a man named Nabal. David needed food for his men; so he sent a handful of men to ask Nabal to feed them. But Nabal insulted David's envoys and refused the favor. David was furious when he heard about Nabal's rudeness. He told his men (all six hundred of them) to strap on their swords and prepare to take out every man in Nabal's household.

Fortunately for Nabal, he was married to the wise and beautiful Abigail. And when Abigail heard about Nabal's refusal to help David and David's proposed harm to the household, she hit the panic button—appropriately. The Bible records that she "made haste" to prepare a huge dinner for the army of six hundred (v. 18). (Can you even imagine?) She hurried out to meet David with the offering and fell at David's feet with apologies for Nabal. And David, to her relief, changed his mind.

> And David said to Abigail, "Blessed be the LORD, the God of Israel, who sent you this day to meet me! Blessed be your discretion, and blessed be you, who have kept me this day from bloodguilt and from avenging myself with my own hand! For as surely as the LORD the God of Israel lives, who has restrained me from hurting you, unless you had hurried and come to meet me, truly by morning there had not been left to Nabal so much as one male." (vv. 32-34, emphasis mine)

In Abigail's case, there was a real emergency—an imminent threat against her family. There was an adequate reason for hurry. She punched the alarm at the appropriate time for the appropriate reason. And her family and servants sprang into action, helping her respond to the emergency. Their haste not only saved the lives of Nabal and his family—it saved David from himself . . . and earned Abigail a blessing.

> **Clearly, you and I are the thermostats in the home. By our very presence, we regulate the temperature of our family and therefore control the atmosphere in our homes. Properly set, we can—by our attitude and actions—meet the specific need of a given moment. (Lindsey O'Connor)**

Would you consider letting Abigail's discernment be your own? When there is real harm facing your family, hurrying may well be the appropriate answer. But if you are speeding along, pushing the panic button, living a life of false emergencies, your greenspanning may well be *causing* harm to your family—keeping stress levels elevated, creating unnecessary anger and frustration, building resentment. Worst of all, you may be training your children to panic inappropriately as well.

Proverbs 22:6 is true: "Train up a child in the way he should go; even when he is old he will not depart from it." But the negative of that statement holds also: Our faulty training tends to stay in our children's lives as well. What you are doing today, right or wrong, is training. If you live a tornado lifestyle, full of perceived but unreal emergencies, you can count on the fact that you are training your child toward a similar adulthood. If getting the house picked up for guests is reason to get histrionic, there's a chance you'll pass that habit along to your kids. If going on a ski-trip vacation creates a hurried, anxious attitude, well, the kids will think that is normal.

However, if you determine to make wise choices about what deserves hurry and when panic is appropriate, your kids will pick that up too. You're likely to have well-adjusted children and a happier husband to boot.

So pray about your perspective. Ask for discernment. Use some discretion and slow down.

No matter what we might think, God's really the one in charge of what's going on in the world.

And with God in control, is there ever a need to panic?

## Time Out

• List a few of the ways you tend to greenspan panic in your life. Are there any recurring themes arising for why and when you do this?

• Looking at your greenspan list, identify the core values that your panics tend to reveal. (For example, when I was panicking over the house getting picked up, I was communicating to my family that appearances are extremely important.)

• Upon identifying those core values, ask yourself: Are they an accurate reflection of who you want you and your family to be?

• Write out a checklist of what describes a real emergency. Place it in a prominent place—perhaps your refrigerator door—as a reminder to use your greenspanning powers wisely.

• Outline a few specific ideas for positive greenspanning, using your influence to make your home a more peaceful, joyful place.

# 13

# Stupid Satan Tricks:

## The Trap of "Time Deprivation"

"**If only I had more time!**" We've probably all made that complaint when we're feeling overloaded.

We look at our crowded calendar or our insistent wristwatch and wistfully consider how great it would be to have more hours available in our days. We "if only" ourselves to death, knowing we would be the people we desire to be if only we had more time. We'd be better people in all the areas of our life. But alas, there is just no way to reach that grand goal, so we're just stuck with this puny portion of time and no way to escape the fact that we will inevitably disappoint someone for our lack of time. We just can't help it. We're time-deprived!

We also feel as though somehow we lose time, as if others were stealing our time or wasting it. The car in front of us is abiding by the speed limit, and we're in a hurry. They've caused us to lose time, and we're furious about it. Our children dawdle in the morning before school. "Hurry up! You're wasting my time. Get going or we're going to be late!" Then we *are* late, and we're sure it's the kids' fault. The guy at the grocery store is scanning too slowly, bagging too carelessly, and talking to his coworker. This infuriates us because we need our time. We covet our time. If we could buy more time we would. We get frantic and stressed out, blaming the slowpokes around us for wasting our time. We feel like we're at the mercy of the clock and all the people around us, and we hate that. But what can we do about it?

What we can do is change the way we think about time in the first place.

The truth is, "time deprivation" is a lie. It's what I playfully call a stupid Satan trick. Not one of us on this grand green earth is deprived of time. And not one of us can control time either. Each day each of us is given the same twenty-four hours. It's our choices that limit us, not our time.

The insidious thing about time-deprivation thinking is that it implies God has somehow cheated us out of our capacity to be our best. He has handicapped us by giving us too much to do and too little time to do it in. The reason our stress is high and we can't get it all done is because we have somehow been robbed of success since we don't have enough tick-tock on the clock. If God is the grand master of time and space, surely He should be able to do something about this viral epidemic of time deprivation (by giving us a little more of it than everybody else). And we stomp our little foot on the floor and crumble into the lie.

In his book *Today Matters* John Maxwell gives a "timely" response to those of us who think we are time-deprived:

> Have you ever found yourself thinking, I need more time? Well, you're not going to get it! No one gets more time. There are 1,440 minutes in a day. No matter what you do, you won't get more time today. Sales consultant and author Myers Barnes says, "Time management has nothing to do with the clock, but everything to do with organizing and controlling your participation in certain events that coordinate with the clock. Einstein understood time management is an oxymoron. It cannot be managed. You can't save time, lose time, turn back the hands of time or have more time tomorrow than today. Time is unemotional, uncontrolled, unencumbered. It moves forward regardless of circumstances and, in the game of life, creates a level playing field for everyone." Since you can't change time, you must instead change your approach to it.[1]

Feeling a little deflated? If time deprivation is indeed a myth and time management is an oxymoron, then there go all our great excuses.

## Stupid Satan Tricks:
## The Trap of "Time Deprivation"

No more blaming the time-distracted dummies in our life. Well, what are we to do?

The first step is to realize that that the real source of our time stress is not a shortage of time. It's not people who waste "our time." It's not even our own faulty time management—because there is really no such thing as managing time. All we can really do is manage our goals and priorities, our activities and commitments, in *light* of our time. The real time stress in our lives comes from *faulty choices* about how we spend the time that God has given us to us.

**To gain a new perspective, our questions must be simple and profound. What is important? Who is important? What are we going to do about it? (Don Osgood)**

The second step, then, is to realize that we make these choices on the basis of our priorities—what is most important to us. And the priorities that actually drive our decisions may well not be the ones that we consciously espouse—or that God wants us to have. And here's a crucial point: *To the extent that your spoken priorities and your daily calendar oppose each other, you will feel defeated, guilty, and most likely time-deprived.*

For example, if I *say* that God is my first priority, but I don't *act* on it (read my Bible and pray, act on the promptings of the Holy Spirit, obey God's commands), chances are, I will feel condemned. My own calendar makes me a liar. If I tell you that I love my husband and he is my first priority, but I am too tired to spend quality time with him, then I am living a lie and will feel constantly condemned by my hypocrisy. If I tell you that I love my children and that their needs come before my own, but I don't make time to care for them, I will live under the weight of my own double-mindedness.

I am convinced that the majority of the stress we feel is the weight of such faulty thinking, the deception of this stupid Satan trick. After all, if the devil can keep us deceived and stressed, he can sabotage our ability to enjoy life and the people we love.

How do we escape the snare? By realizing that our true priorities are revealed by the things we actually *do* with our lives, not the things we *say* we value. Our priorities are the things we spend our money on, not the things we say we'd like to spend money on.

"Well, I'd like to tithe, but we just don't have the money to squeeze out of our budget."

"I'd love to visit my sick mother-in-law, but with work and the kids, I just can't find the time."

Our priorities speak for themselves. They are not really hidden, though our own self-deception and wishful thinking can hide them from ourselves. We manage to find time to eat (plenty of that), but we're too wiped out to exercise. We find time to chat on the phone and share our "Christian concerns" about our friends, but we can't find time to pray for them. We'll gripe about the teachers at school in the carpool line, but we don't have time to make an appointment and speak with them privately about our issues. We find plenty of time to buy more than we can afford but can't find the time to care for all the stuff.

Stupid Satan tricks—all of them. Wake up and smell the coffee, my tired, frazzled friend. You may not be able to manage your time, but you are definitely managing your choices according to your priorities, even if those priorities aren't exactly what you thought they were.

And the really good news is, if you don't like your choices, you can change them.

That is exactly what I had to do when I realized I was griping about my time troubles to my husband. We had come to a budgetary meeting of the minds and established that either we had to change our standard of living by cutting expenses or I needed to get a part-time job. Instead of letting go of our favorite (expensive) sports activity, horseback riding, I decided that if God provided a job, I would take it. Well, God literally dropped an awesome ministry position in my lap. It fit in with my family priorities and my dreams about my life. So I took the job, and I loved it. But after the first couple of days, I was complaining to my husband about all the new stress this God-sent job entailed.

"I don't have enough time to get it all done," I whined, "and my stomach is killing me because I am so freaked out about all I have to do." Wah, wah, wah . . . poor, pitiful me.

Now, my husband is one of the kindest, most sympathetic men in the world. So it really surprised me when Will said, "If your life is making you sick, then change it."

I stood in shocked silence, but I knew he was right. I backed off quickly and said not another complaining word.

Is your life and your schedule making you sick? Then perhaps you should change what you are doing.

If you think your priorities are off-kilter, you can change those too.

And if you really believe your choices and your priorities are on target and you cannot imagine changing them, then there's always the option of changing your attitude.

That's because sometimes our time troubles aren't really a matter of misplaced priorities. Sometimes they're just a matter of forgetting that every goal and dream comes with a time and energy price tag attached.

Recently I was talking with a friend who is in a very busy season in her life. She is realizing a professional dream that she has hoped and prayed about for many years. When I talked with her, she was complaining about the many people who wanted her time, seeking her out for advice and wisdom. I gently reminded her that she was getting exactly what she'd prayed for—to be sought after for advice—and that the attention was a piece of the price for achieving her professional dream.

It's funny how confused we can get over our priorities and the price we must pay to see them come to fruition. I prayed to become a mother, and yet the time and maintenance involved in mothering is sometimes a source of complaint. I have longed to author a book, a lifelong dream, and yet I can sometimes be found muttering and complaining about the pressure of deadlines. I love being married and longed for marriage as a young girl, but you might hear me gripe about the effort it takes to live in harmony with my husband.

Complaining, of course, is often just a way of letting off steam. It's not necessarily harmful in itself—unless we embrace the negativism and allow it to take root in our hearts. But it's so easy to do that once we get into the habit of whining about our lives. Our complaints can really mask our stubborn refusal to accept the price tag for our goals and dreams—to admit that anything truly valuable will cost us something in terms of time and energy.

# The Time of Your Life

**We must learn to realize that the love of God seeks us in every situation, and seeks our good. (Thomas Merton)**

Jesus urged right thinking about this when He said, "For which of you, desiring to build a tower, does not first sit down and count the cost, whether he has enough to complete it?" (Luke 14:28). That is what priority management is really all about. If we desire to live a sane and balanced life, then we absolutely must begin to realize the connection between a priority or goal and the cost associated with obtaining it. We must honestly consider what it will take to pursue that priority or goal within the framework of available time and energy—and in the light of what God wants for our lives.

This last element is especially important because God has gifted us with time in the first place so we can live out His will on earth. This has to be the first priority for any believer, and living by other priorities will always be a time and energy drain. The truth is, if God has placed dreams in our hearts and a call upon our lives, He is able to fulfill them. There is no lack of time where God is concerned. Elisabeth Elliot in *Discipline: The Glad Surrender* puts it this way:

> *There is always enough time to do the will of God.* For that we can never say, "I don't have enough time." When we find ourselves frantic and frustrated, harried and harassed and "hassled," it is a sign that we are running on our own schedule, not on God's.[2]

I have to agree with that. I have found that I frequently give myself more hours in my day than are humanly possible. I load up on goals without adequately counting the cost, and then I'm dismayed to discover I've "run out of time." Then I end up frustrated, griping about my lack of time and all I have to accomplish.

Did God set me up to fail? Of course not. God does not fail. I fail. I fail to count the cost. I fail to understand that time is not managed—priorities are managed. I fail to understand what is realistic for my life and for my family, and so I make bad choices. I fail to make God's will my first priority and thus rob myself of the energy that comes from living in Him.

I am the one. Not God, not others, but me.

God, on the other hand, is sufficient and able. He always desires to help me and to teach me about choices and priorities, about His great plans for my life and about the energy boost that comes from spending "my time" His way. That is what God is busy about. "I know the thoughts and plans that I have for you," He tells us, "thoughts and plans for welfare and peace and not for evil, to give you hope in your final outcome" (Jeremiah 29:11-13, AMP).

Do you feel caught in a time crunch that has you fussing and fuming? Do you long for more hours in your day, more days in your week, more weeks in your year? Do you long for more peace, more simplicity, more joyful living?

Then open your mind and your heart to God's plans for peace—real daily peace in the midst of the traffic jams and the grocery store lanes and the off-to-school rush. Let Him change your thinking and shape your choices and sweeten your attitude.

You will find plans unfolding that give God's great hope for your life.

# Time Out

• What specific circumstances in your life tend to try your patience and make you wish for "more time"?

• Look carefully at your schedule, and try to identify some activities that reflect an unspoken priority. What does your weekly schedule say about your values in life?

• What is one of your biggest dreams in life—either for the present or the future? What time and energy price is associated with that dream?

• List a goal you have for yourself this month. Specify the actual time and energy that accomplishing that goal will require.

• List at least three changes you can make in the next month—choices, priorities, or attitude—that could help reduce the time stress in your life.

# 14

# Peer Pressure for Grown-ups:

## The Trap of People Pleasing

**Peer pressure**—it's not just for teenagers anymore!

In fact, I believe many of our problems as modern women—especially our time crunches—arise from the fact that we are driven by others' perceptions about our lives and choices. In some sense we are still hoping to be voted "best all around." So we try to tune our lives to others' thinking and their priorities, leaving our own priorities by the wayside and wasting precious time and energy.

You don't think this applies to you? Well, maybe. But I know that I'm not immune to people pleasing. I doubt that many of us are.

For example, most moms would agree that one of our main jobs is to look out for our children's best interests. But when all of Johnny's friends are going out for Pop Warner football and Johnny isn't interested, you might start to think something's wrong with Johnny. Maybe the other kids will pick on him if he doesn't play. Maybe we should insist . . .

Or maybe the minister's wife (not me!) has asked you to lead a Bible study in your home. And you'd really like to do it—someday. But right now you just don't have the time, the energy, or the sense that God is calling you to this particular ministry. Still, you don't want to disappoint her.

Or maybe a group of friends has decided it would be fun to go out to dinner once a week. And it would be fun . . . if you had the budget for it and an extra night in your week. But if you say no, will they still meet you for coffee?

And so we end up pushing Johnny into football (and cringing on the sidelines when he flinches from the ball). We agree to the Bible study and lose two afternoons we can't afford—one cleaning and one hosting. We do our best with the dinner club, though our heart isn't in it. And the list goes one. We chair the fund-raiser because "they really need me." Or we drag ourselves out to the garden despite the fact that we hate gardening because "everyone in this neighborhood grows flowers." We say yes to our boss's overtime expectations, take an extra job to afford the private school everyone else says is best, and then frantically try to make time for the commitments that matter most to us . . . and to God.

Please understand—I'm not saying that any of these activities, in themselves, are bad. Football and fund-raisers, Bible studies and gardening, overtime and dinner groups, playgroups and private schools can all be worthwhile choices. The problem is doing them for the wrong reasons.

**I don't know the key to success, but the key to failure is trying to please everybody else. (Bill Cosby)**

When meeting outside expectations supersedes more appropriate priorities in life, trouble inevitably bubbles up. Appropriate priorities are based not on the opinions of other people but on true wisdom, the kind of wisdom found in the Bible. Galatians 1:10 reveals this wisdom by reminding us who we ultimately need to please in our lives. "Am I now trying to win the approval of men, or of God? . . . If I were still trying to please men, I would not be a servant of Christ" (NIV).

For Christians, this concept of pleasing God first should seem obvious. So should the concept that we should make choices in light of what our family needs, not what outsiders think. But practically speaking, the stress of outside pressures and demands can be immense.

Even grown-ups, after all, feel the need to fit in, and we want our children to fit in as well. We want friends who love us and admire us. We want to be useful, to be respected, to be affirmed and applauded. And frankly, a lot of family tasks can feel thankless and unappreciated. (How long has it been since one of your children gave you a pat on the back and told you, "Good job, Mom"?)

We know that our worth as women and as people should not be based on what others think about us—or about what we would *like* them to think about us. We know we shouldn't base our decisions on what others expect. And yet it's so easy to fall into that time-wasting trap of being a people pleaser, letting others' perceptions and opinions shape our choices.

Trying to live up to the never-ending invisible standards of our social, work, and school worlds inevitably leads to stress and burnout because of the tension between what we think we should do, what we truly want to do, and what we're actually doing—not to mention the effort of cramming too much activity into a twenty-four-hour day. Our spirit may be screaming out for freedom and peace, but we continue our people-pleasing behavior for fear of disappointing someone. What will they think of us if we don't do what they want?

If you find yourself constantly on edge and exhausted, I'd like to suggest an experiment. Set aside a time when you can actually find a little quiet. Pray for wisdom. Then write out a long list of your current obligations—your own and your family's—and ask yourself these questions about each one of them:

• Is this activity something I actually *want* to do?

• Am I participating in it out of a sense of obligation to anyone other than God and my family?

• Am I requiring my family to participate in this out of obligation?

• Does this activity fill a void in my life that really needs to be filled by God?

• Does it get in the way of my most important relationships?

• Does this commitment overload my schedule and cause me to feel restless, exhausted, or irritated on a regular basis?

Deep inside, you know which commitments in your life are putting on the pressure, which ones were made for the wrong reasons. The Spirit of God who is in us rallies against the minor issues we love to make the main issues in our lives. God jealously fights on our behalf for proper perspective. He desires that His priorities become our priorities.

Jesus cautioned us not to make worry a mainstay—and what is obsession with others' perceptions but another form of worry? Hear what He has to say in Matthew 6:25: "Do not be anxious about your life, what you will eat or what you will drink, nor about your body, what you will put on. Is not life more than food, and the body more than clothing?" I like to paraphrase this for the modern mom: "Now listen, don't fret about you and your family doing all the 'right' things—playing every sport, providing every music lesson, joining the acceptable clubs, being seen at *the* social events, vacationing with certain friends. Aren't you, your husband, and your kids worth more than that? Don't stress about it. Don't let your calendar overrun your priorities."

**Obviously, I'm not trying to be a people pleaser! No, I am trying to please God. If I were still trying to please people, I would not be Christ's servant. (Galatians 1:10, NLT)**

Instead of excessive preoccupation with the Joneses, try Jesus' prescription for the anxious agenda: "But seek first the kingdom of God and his righteousness, and all these things will be added to you" (Matthew 6:33). Make God's priorities yours by agreeing to seek His kingdom in your life and in the life of your family every day. While you are in the arenas of obligation such as work and school, you must be ever aware of guarding your priorities. Diligently protect what matters most in your life. Do not let what other people think or ask you to do become your foremost preoccupation. Instead, let God's plan and purposes be what drives your decision-making.

Oswald Chambers wrote in regard to spending time and evaluating priorities, "It is not the thing we spend the most time on that molds us most; the greatest element is the thing that exerts most power. We must determine to be limited and concentrate our affinities."[1] I like that idea of concentrating our affinities. It implies an emphasis on quality rather than quantity, focusing our main energies on activities that support what we care about most.

## Peer Pressure for Grown-ups:
## The Trap of People Pleasing

What are you concentrating on? Is it what others think of you, or is it what God wants in your life? Honestly answer: What exerts the most power over your schedule? If you are joyless and dissatisfied, perhaps it is because much of what you're doing is unrelated to your true priorities. Maybe you are picking up loads God never intended for you to carry.

If you are adding loads of toil to your already loaded plate, you are probably unhappy. Why not consider getting out of something? There is no shame in dropping out, quitting, or breaking a commitment that you cannot justify in light of your priorities, especially an obligation made under the duress of others' expectations. Most people will accept your decision and move on. If they don't—well, the benefit of sanity is worth risking the displeasure of a judgmental acquaintance.

I remember pulling out of a position as a homeroom mom at my child's school. The school year had already started, and my spirit was squawking away. I felt constantly anxious and irritated, and I knew I had accepted the position without counting the cost to my family. I pulled Roxann, the woman in charge, aside and told her I could not fulfill my commitment. I was embarrassed. I even teared up because I like to be thought of as a responsible and reliable person. The whole experience was very humbling.

But Roxann was so gracious. She told me not to worry. She did not shame or blame, and she handled the whole situation like a real grown-up. Some weeks later, in fact, she pulled me aside to tell me how much she admired what I did and how she hoped she would be willing to do the same for her family. And Roxann is one of my dearest friends today.

Learning to live according to appropriate priorities—God's priorities—will nurture your self-confidence and free your spirit. It will teach you the benefits of making good choices and help you grow in wisdom. You will reap impressive benefits in terms of time, energy, and serenity. And other people's reactions may surprise you. You may find that the people you worried about letting down are fine with your decision—or are at least willing to respect it. You may even discover, as I did, that your integrity about your priorities and your schedule enhances your relationships with people whose friendship is worth cultivating. When people understand that God and your family are your first priorities and they encourage you in that, grab hold of those people. They are the folks with whom you need to be in relationship.

That doesn't mean *everyone* will applaud you for sticking to your guns. Some may feel hurt or let down. Some may criticize you or gossip behind your back. People who try to make you feel guilty about not living up to their expectations are usually people with their own problems. They may be insecure in their own choices or struggling with their priorities. Or they may think you are the answer to all their needs. But you're not really responsible for other people's reaction. Just explain your decisions graciously and try to back out of obligations with as little damage as possible. After that, whether it is your boss, your best friend, your children's minister, or even your mother expecting you to conform to his or her expectations, you need to stand firm. Your first priority is to be responsive to God's call on your life, which includes your responsibilities to your family and your own growth.

Your call is to please God, not others.

So make your decisions, leave the rest to Him . . . and luxuriate in the joy of a schedule that lets you breathe.

## Time Out

• How many items could you remove from your week if you felt you wouldn't be letting anyone down?

• In what ways might you be (unconsciously) teaching your child to please others rather than to please God?

• Take a look at your schedule for the week. What do your most time-consuming activities tell you about whom you want to please?

• What are direct emotional manifestations of a people-pleasing schedule?

• List the reasons you try to "win the approval of men" (Galatians 1:10, NIV).

• How could you adjust your schedule to more accurately reflect that you are living life to win the approval of God?

# 15

# Maggots in the Manna:

## The Trap of Discontentment

**I regard God as the** ultimate creative genius, but there are a few of His creatures that I sometimes wonder about. For example, I have a hard time understanding the function of a cockroach. While some entomologist might expound on the worthwhile nature of the roach, I am quite sure that this insect's function in life is to totally and utterly gross people out. A second creature that I have trouble with is the maggot. Even writing the word causes me to gasp. I've been told that these sick little creatures can actually be beneficial to the environment, but to me they are nauseating little creatures with which I desire no interaction.

That said, I'm guessing you could imagine what I felt like when, much to my disgust, I found hundreds of the twisting creatures on my garage floor. Apparently someone had deposited a food item in the open trash can in the garage one hot summer day and forgot about emptying it. Within a few days, a smart fly laid about a billion eggs and guess what? They all hatched in my garage. The stench was unbearable, but to me the biggest problem was that I was the only one home to exterminate the creatures. I squealed and jumped and held my breath, desperately trying to kill them all with Windex spray (the closest chemical available), praying all the time that I wouldn't faint on the floor and get permanently invaded.

# The Time of Your Life

It was a grotesque experience, one I never hope to repeat. And I'm sure the Israelites' encounter with maggots was just as gross. In their case, it was all about discontentment and the desire for more.

We read in Exodus 16 that the Israelites found themselves tired and discontented in the desert. Not long after God rescued them from their oppression in Egypt, they started complaining to Moses, their leader.

*"Oh, that we were back in Egypt," they moaned, "It would have been better if the LORD had killed us there! At least there we had plenty to eat. But now you have brought us into this desert to starve to death." (v. 3, NLT)*

Their grumbling led God to provide some extra food in a most unusual and miraculous way.

*Then the LORD said to Moses, "Look, I'm going to rain down food from heaven for you. The people can go out each day and pick up as much food as they need for that day. I will test them in this to see whether they will follow my instructions." (v. 4, NLT, emphasis mine)*

The Lord kept His promise, providing quail in the evening and manna in the morning. But when the manna appeared, the Israelites were puzzled by its appearance.

*"What is it?" they asked. And Moses told them, "It is the food the LORD has given you. The LORD says that each household should gather as much as it needs." (vv. 15-16, NLT, emphasis mine)*

Moses passed along God's warning:

*"Do not keep any of it overnight." But of course, some of them didn't listen and kept some of it until morning. By then it was full of maggots and had a terrible smell. And Moses was very angry with them. (vv. 19-20, NLT)*

Why did Moses get angry with the Israelites? Because they had failed the test God set before them.

And the name of that pop quiz? Contentment.

## Maggots in the Manna:
## The Trap of Discontentment

I hate that test. I have failed it on many occasions. Contentment is about being satisfied with what you have. It is about settling down with gratitude to what God has provided. And for some reason that's really hard for most of us.

It certainly was for the Israelites. God tested them by asking them to only get *what they needed for that day*. And Moses, ever the dutiful teaching assistant, passed along those instructions very clearly. But still they failed the test.

Now, you may think, *Those silly, ungrateful Israelites. The food would have been there tomorrow. Why couldn't they just trust in what God had promised!* Yes, I too am somewhat amused at the Israelites and their continual distrust of God's promise—the ongoing grumbling, the incessant whining. And yet I know that had I been there in the desert with them, I might have tried to take a little more than I needed and save it for tomorrow . . . just in case. I would likely have failed the contentment pop quiz right along with the Israelites, just as I have failed it in my lifetime.

Did you know that discontentment has a lot to do with feeling time-deprived? That's what an article from *Newsweek* implies:

> Getting wealthier spawns other complaints. One is the "time squeeze"—the sense that we're more harried than ever. We all know this is true; we're tugged by jobs, by family, PTA and soccer. Actually, it's not true. People go to work later in life and retire earlier. Housework has declined. One survey found that in 1999 only 14 percent of wives did more that four hours of daily housework; the figure was 43 percent in 1977 and 87 percent in 1924. Even when jobs and housework are combined, total work hours for women and men have dropped.
>
> Still, people gripe—and griping rises with income, report economists Daniel Hamermesh of the University of Texas and Jungmin Lee of the University of Arkansas. They studied the United States, Germany, Australia, Canada, and South Korea. People who were otherwise statistically similar (same age, working hours, number of children) complained more about the "time squeeze" as their incomes rose. Hamermesh and Lee's explanation: the more money people have, the more things they can do with their time; time

becomes more valuable, and people increasingly resent that they can't create more of it.[1]

You could be reading and thinking, *Well, that's not me, because I am certainly not wealthy*. But I have two questions.

First, do you feel you have enough time?

And second, do you wake up wanting? You know—after you've had your first cup of coffee and you move out into the morning, is there a possibility that your mental list of things to do includes a lot of things you want?

**I believe that hell will be a frantic, desperate place where people are clutching what they own and grabbing for more. But heaven will be a place where our hands can no longer make greedy little fists. (Claire Cloninger)**

You think, *I'd like to run by Starbucks and get a latte*. Or as you pull into the parking lot at work or school you glance at the car next to you. *I sure would like to drive that car*. Maybe you see a friend who is nicely dressed, and you think, *Wow, I need to do some shopping*.

I think that way sometimes. It is as natural to me as breathing. And I've noticed a tendency to keep wanting just a little more, and a little more after that. It's an easy next step from there to acting on my wants. And before I know it, I'm filling my time with buying, storing, and collecting instead of being happy with what I have—and feeling more and more hurried and harried in the process.

So I know that article applies to me. Discontentment breeds more discontentment—and the illusion that there just isn't enough of anything, time included, to take care of my needs.

Every year, spring and fall, I take a short day trip to a town called Round Top, which hosts one of the nation's largest antique shows. Alongside the antiques are tables lined with all sorts of junk. It's a treasure hunter's paradise because sometimes you can sneak out with a real bargain.

Every year that I go, without exception, I feel ambivalent toward the shopping. I don't really need anything, but I go because I love the experience. I love wandering the maze of tables with a friend. I get a thrill out of digging up great buys. So every year I come home with the car piled with stuff I didn't know I wanted or needed, and I am hungry to go back the very next day. For me, Round Top is a breeding ground for discontentment.

Now, please don't hear me say that shopping is inherently wrong. I enjoy my fair share of shopping. But there has to be a stopping point. Just as for most people there is a feeling of fullness when eating, a time when your stomach tightens and you know you've had enough, there is an internal signal that enough is enough. And to disregard that signal within is to lunge ahead into feeding the discontented soul.

I have surely felt that tug inside my soul that says, *Enough buying. Enough shopping. Enough wanting.* In other words, *That's enough manna for you today.*

Have you felt it too? It's there for a reason. But the typical response is to do what many overeaters do with food—to stifle the voice by getting *more*.

It's a classic struggle—two internal voices, one saying, *more*, and the other whispering, *enough*. And the one we choose to listen to makes a big difference in our happiness and our peace.

Did you know that the feelings of struggle over buying more or having more will go away if unfed, if we heed the voice of *enough* and choose to believe that God will richly supply? But the opposite is also true: going after more just breeds more hunger. Hoarding increases the desire to hoard . . . and that's where the maggots come in.

Imagine if I got back in the car (day two) and headed back toward Round Top the minute I had the feeling of needing more. Well, my house would be loaded down with more "treasures" I would end up putting in a garage sale two years down the road. More important, I would probably still be wanting more, because the more we acquire, the louder the voice of discontentment grows.

When we look toward desiring and buying stuff continually, our hearts fall victim to the lie that what we need, including time, is in short supply, that even God might not be able to come through for us. And that in turn actually keeps us very busy. We become like the Israelites, scrambling to take care of ourselves. And what we get as a result is what the Israelites experienced with the maggot-covered manna: life stinks. Life stinks because we are ever striving and churning and spinning as we try to make it all happen on our own—not to mention caring for what we've acquired. And that all takes lots of time . . . adding to the sense of being very busy.

"Beware of the barrenness of a busy life." That's one of those quotes that has been attributed to everybody from Socrates to Corrie ten Boom to Ruth Bell Graham, probably because it rings so true. It speaks directly to the fact that discontentment leads to materialism, and materialism creates more discontentment—a sense of emptiness, of wanting still more. And yet I often lunge ahead blindly and step into the deep hole of discontentment.

So what is the answer for the shopped-out, the worn-out, we who are weary yet still struggle with feelings of discontentment? How can we silence the voice of *more* long enough to heed the assurance of *enough*?

One practical measure is to stay away from the Round Tops in your life, whatever or wherever they may be. Some people find that a very helpful solution. But most women I know, for whom shopping is recreational and also part of our job description in the home, find that avoiding stores is not very realistic. Besides, it's not a sin to enjoy spending what God has given you.

### Defining "enough"—with guidance from the Lord—is indeed key to contentment. (Lindsey O'Connor)

So here's another idea that has helped me a lot. You might not like it—*I* don't always like it. But for me it has worked very well to cure discontentment.

It goes like this: Start giving things away.

"Oh," I hear you saying, "she wants me to clean out my closet and get rid of the things I don't want and don't need." But that is not what I mean. I'm talking about giving away the things you do want and do need, and doing it on a routine basis. That sounds radical. But for me that habit has been an important key to breaking the stronghold of discontentment in my life. It has truly made me a happier, more peaceful person with more joy in my life and more time to do what I really care about.

The truth is, when you want victory in an area of life, you don't compromise with the enemy—you conquer the enemy. That is a spiritual law, the key to getting healthy. And if discontentment is the enemy, then you must understand that the restlessness for more is a form of greed. It's a form of distrust—doubting that the Lord really can and will supply your needs. And to me at least, the best way to break free from that restless wanting is to face down the problem—to turn my two hands over and release it all to God.

Here's how it works for me. Say someone comes over to my house and mentions that she loves something I have, perhaps a fragrant candle I am burning. My general habit is to ask her if she would like to take it with her. Or maybe some friends come over to eat, and one of them goes on and on about what I have made, stating how delicious it is. I pack it up for them to take home. I look for opportunities to allow someone else to enjoy and get pleasure out of "*my* stuff." In the past few years I've given away clothing, books, purses—all sorts of things.

Most of the time, I find, it's satisfying to give my stuff away, at least once I get over the initial urge to snatch it back. Giving makes me feel generous and free and trusting, and it's fun to see the joy my giving provides for others. It's something I've really come to enjoy . . . most of the time.

Once at church I happened to have sixty dollars worth of "mad money" in my purse, money I had set aside for some fun. I felt God prompting me to put that money in the offering bowl. You should have seen me squirm: *No, God. Remember, I already tithed this month. This is money for me to play with, to treat myself to a manicure or a new pair of shoes* . . . I was frantic, trying desperately to hold on to that sixty bucks.

And then I remembered how my habit of giving away has helped me. I also remembered the Israelites and the maggots. Finally I tore into my wallet, got that money out, and tossed it in the bowl before I had the chance to change my mind. It was hard, but I'm glad I did it.

Now please understand, I'm not saying we should give *everything* away. My children aren't in danger of coming home from school and finding the furniture gone. And although two of my close friends (who know of my habit) have told me they just "love my little white Volvo," I have yet to hand over the keys! I try very hard not to let giving become a compulsion for me . . . or a power trip. And yet I do try keep my eyes open every day for opportunities to open my hands to God instead of clenching them around stuff. And the minute I feel the tug to hoard something I really like, I try to thrust it in the opposite direction, knowing the thing has a potential hold on my contentment.

As I have released stuff to others, I have experienced two revelations. The first is, I rarely miss the item that is gone (although I did pout over the sixty bucks for a day). The second is that I have one less object to dust or store or otherwise take up my time. Giving things away, in other words, earns me freedom in space and time.

How much of your life will you take with you when you pass from this world? Why not slow down your mind and your body and enjoy what you have today instead of hammering away at the things that drive you to busyness by causing you to want more?

Learning contentment isn't easy, but the rewards are worth it. More time. More peace. More trust.

And if I never see another maggot in my manna—or anywhere—that's fine with me.

## Time Out

• In what ways is your life stinky because of discontentment? What do you tend to want more of?

• Explain the following equation: More money = more freedom of time = resentment.

• Read 1 Timothy 6:6-8 and explain the following equation: Contentment + Godliness = Great Gain.

• Try this little experiment. Every day for the next week, give something away. It doesn't have to be a material object. For example, while at the grocery store, give away your spot in line to the person behind you. Or pay for someone else's meal (the car behind you) at a drive-through restaurant. Or simply defer by letting others have their way. (It's all giving.) Keep a journal of how you felt and what resulted.

• Read and memorize 2 Corinthians 9:8: "God will generously provide all you need. Then you will always have everything you need and plenty left over to share with others" (NLT).

• How is learning to *receive* graciously and gratefully (from God and from other people) related to this issue of being content?

# 16

# Shortcuts:

## The Trap of Convenience

**All right, I admit it.** I'm a piecrust snob.

I turn my nose up at the "refrigerator fresh" piecrusts at the grocery store. I would never dream of taking a bakery pie or—heaven forbid—something from the freezer to a potluck or a bake sale. And I come by my snobbery honestly; my mother made some of the flakiest, most delicious pies I've ever tasted. I have to tell you, I was shocked at my first taste of the store-bought version. It had none of the homemade tenderness I had grown up loving.

When I was young, I used to sit at my mother's elbow, begging for the scraps of piecrust as she rolled out the dough at Thanksgiving and Christmas. And from the minute I was allowed to experiment in the kitchen, I made it my mission to learn the secrets of those four simple ingredients that make up a pastry shell. Years later I even taught a cooking class for my friends called "Easy as Pie" dedicated to dispelling the myth that mixing together flour, salt, fat, and water is a mystery.

When my friends arrived for my class, I demonstrated that making a pastry shell really is as easy as pie. I had them time me on the clock to prove that making a homemade pie shell was much quicker than driving to the grocery store and picking up one of those despicable, rubbery versions. (See, I told you—a real piecrust snob!) I had them make a shell themselves, hoping to entice them with the ease of the recipe I provided. I even baked a pie there in class, knowing the smell and taste of the chicken potpie with its crumbly, tender crust would convince them to take home this new value—the value of a homemade piecrust.

I believe it, and I've proved it many times—producing a tender, flaky, delectable homemade crust really is as easy as pie. Yet even I have to admit that buying a refrigerator piecrust can be very convenient. And convenience, I've learned, is a very popular thing.

Think about it. We have convenience foods—frozen dinners, take-out meals, fast-food. We have convenience stores—milk, gas, and dog food, all in one easy (but expensive) stop. All manner of service industries, from dog-sitters to personal shoppers, offer us convenient ways to take care of our responsibilities. We schedule appointments on the basis of convenience and look for convenient ways to get to and from work and school. Every single day most of us weigh convenience as a factor in every decision.

**Good planning and hard work lead to prosperity, but hasty shortcuts lead to poverty. (Proverbs 21:5, NLT)**

Except in matters of piecrust, I'm not really opposed to convenience. I think it can actually be a very good thing, a way of making time for what is most important. But what happens when our quest for convenience pushes us to take shortcuts on important issues? Now that can cause some problems.

While hiking in Colorado, I've often noticed signs on steep mountain trails: "Stay on the trail." "No shortcuts." Why such stern words? The answer has to do with switchbacks—and with our culture's chronic quest for convenience.

Switchbacks are the zigzag, sideways patterns the trails take as they snake up the mountains. The switchbacks reduce the grade of the climb, and they are also carefully designed to create a stable path that eliminates trail erosion. But many hikers dislike following the switchbacks because they take a little longer. These hurried people find it more convenient to take shortcuts straight up or down the mountain, breaking through the foliage instead of following the designated (and clearly marked) path.

It's understandable why hikers would choose to create their own shortcuts. Doing so reduces actual hiking distance and gets them to their destination faster. But hikers who take these types of shortcuts are not only breaking the posted rules and endangering themselves by taking on steeper inclines—they are also violating trail etiquette.

*Etiquette,* of course, is just another word for manners. It is a code of conduct based on a set of principles. In the case of hiking, the code of conduct involves protecting the natural environment and allowing others to benefit from its beauty after you are gone. Trail etiquette exists to preserve the trail and the hiking experience for everyone.

So what in the world does this have to do with time, convenience, and shortcuts?

In our culture, just about everything because our preoccupation with convenience can cause us to take shortcuts that violate important principles. We go for what is easy instead of what is right. And the result is similar to what happens when hikers violate trail etiquette.

The result is *erosion.*

When we continually cut corners in terms of manners and thoughtfulness, we erode the general level of civility in our culture. When we take the easy way out morally, we erode the ethical codes that keep society stable. When we opt for convenience in our spiritual practices, our spiritual awareness and maturity suffers. And taking shortcuts in the way we treat others—something that is all too common in our materialistic, convenience-loving society—inevitably erodes both our intimate relationships and the civility of our interactions with people on the street.

Jesus said, "Whatever you wish that others would do to you, do also to them, for this is the Law and the Prophets" (Matthew 7:12). With this famous Golden Rule, He was laying down a guiding principle for building right relationships: Do the thing you'd like done to you. Why did He tell us that so specifically? Because our natural, selfish tendency is to do whatever we want to do, whatever is easiest. Satisfying our personal desires just feels good. But Jesus' very next sentence is most interesting: "Enter by the narrow gate. For the gate is wide and the way easy that leads to destruction, and those who enter by it are many. For the gate is narrow and the way is hard that leads to life, and those who find it are few" (v. 13).

In the original context, Jesus was relating Himself to the narrow gate, presenting Himself as the only way to heaven. But this verse also tells us something about shortcuts. Jesus points out that the easy way or the convenient way often leads to destruction, or erosion, if you will—lots of people hiking that shortcut, breaking the underbrush, loosening the topsoil. The narrow way, the harder way, the zigzagging path up the mountain, may take a little longer, but it is the life-filled way. It is the way to nurture and preserve what is worth having in life.

What am I getting at? Just this: when we make convenience our guiding principle where people are concerned, we tend to cut corners with people. We fail to greet a neighbor at the supermarket because we're really in a hurry. We miss an appointment with a friend and let it go with a muttered apology. We set the kids in front of the TV with a pizza in place of actually setting the table and sitting down for an actual family dinner. We give up on getting everyone out of bed, dressed, and off to church.

**The heart of all good manners is the Golden Rule: Do unto others as you would have them do unto you. (Emilie Barnes)**

And what is the immediate result of little shortcuts like these? In the short run, to be honest, not much. Destruction by erosion rarely happens in a day or even a year. But the long-term result of many little shortcuts is a washed-out hillside: alienated neighbors, estranged friendships, families that drift apart, spiritual commitments that fall by the wayside. Not to mention a culture whose moral and ethical code seems to be dissolving day by day. The effect, in other words, is cumulative.

And what does that have to do with time? Just about everything. It has to do with *quality and quantity*. Quality refers to how good something is. Quantity refers to a number or amount. And while debates rage on about quality time versus quantity time, the truth is, they are entangled. There are no real shortcuts where people are concerned. Quality relationships are difficult to come by without investing a certain quantity of time. Even basic civility requires a certain investment of time—time that more and more people in our society seem unwilling to spend.

Here's a very simple illustration. The next time you are in the grocery store parking lot, notice how people in cars treat pedestrians. The law always gives the pedestrians the right of way. And yet I have been flabbergasted to watch people in cars nearly run over pedestrians who are attempting to get full carts of groceries to their car. I have seen frail elderly women scrambling to avoid impatient drivers.

Rushing to beat pedestrians instead of allowing them the right of way in the parking lot is a destructive kind of shortcut, an erosive form of convenience. These parking lot bullies only gain maybe five or ten seconds by not yielding. But otherwise polite people are willing to do almost anything for the sake of a shortcut.

Or what about stoplights at an intersection? The yellow light typically means yield, caution, slow—but apparently not where I live. Here the amber light seems to be a signal for many drivers to take a shortcut, to put the pedal to the metal and push through the light before it turns red. That's exactly what happened to my hair stylist. Her car was totaled by a man trying to shortcut the light. She found herself in the hospital for two months recuperating, lucky to be alive. Essentially that man traded two months of a woman's life for his two minutes saved in traffic. He thought it would be more convenient to run the light and save some time. As her medical bills mount (which he has to pay), I wonder if he still feels the same way.

Do we just not have time for thoughtfulness anymore, for kindness or consideration or basic respect? Do we rush frantically, consumed with our time and oblivious to others' needs? What kind of erosion happens when our time crunches cause us to treat others with neglect or contempt?

I wonder about our collective desire to live quick and convenient lives. I believe our lack of reflective thinking puts us in a position of just reacting to the demands of our own lives instead of letting principle drive our behavior. *Quick, fast,* and *now* seem to be our only watchwords. In our hunger for shortcuts, "Do unto others as you would have them do unto you" is easily tossed aside.

What's the remedy? Well, there's a lot to be said for taking the narrow road, the long way, the switchback trail, especially in the way we treat people. That means taking the time for some courtesy, for some thoughtfulness. It means recognizing that though your time is precious, so is your neighbor's. It means resisting the temptation to save time by cutting corners on your principles. It means making sure your conduct reflects biblical standards no matter how inconvenient that conduct may be at the moment.

Reflecting biblical standards in this culture takes thoughtfulness and, yes, it takes time. Principled living is not always convenient. But even in our convenience-obsessed culture, the narrow, slower road is still the path to life, and "doing unto others as I would have them do unto me" is still the Golden Rule.

You really might not be interested in making a homemade piecrust. I respect that, even though homemade crust really is delicious and not that hard, really. But piecrust (or hiking) won't really make that much difference to eternity.

But your relationships will.

Your character will.

Your principles will.

What makes the biggest difference in the long run is how much you trust the Lord and how well you manage to love others. And in these areas, as in piecrust, there are really no shortcuts.

## Time Out

• List some examples of shortcuts you commonly take that save time in a positive way.

• List a few examples of shortcuts you have taken that could eventually erode your principles or your relationships.

• Name at least one example from your life where you believe quantity (the amount of time you spent) affected the quality of an experience or relationship. How do you think the two are interrelated?

## Shortcuts:
## The Trap of Convenience

• What signs of erosion in the area of your principles or relationships result when you take the path of least resistance?

• In what areas of your life are you most likely to cut corners of thoughtfulness or civility? What do you think this says about your values?

# 17

# Running from the Truth:

## The Trap of Toxic Busyness

**It was a rainy morning** in Georgia when Lisa sat down next to me, her eyes averted. She stared silently out the streaming window while I waited for her to tell me what was on her mind.

She had requested to speak with me after a keynote address I'd given at a conference. Professional, successful, and seemingly confident, she surprised me with her speechlessness. "What's going on?" I finally asked her. Tears streamed down her face. "I hate myself. I'm a horrible person." She could barely finish her sentences. What in the world was going on in her head? She had the countenance of a scorned child.

After much conversation, Lisa confessed a marital affair some seven months previous. She was terrified to tell her husband, for fear he would leave her and take their only child with him. Unconfessed sin and condemnation pressed heavily on her heart and mind and even her body. She described symptom after symptom, and none surprised me but one. In her sleeplessness, she had developed a habit of exercising. In the early hours of the morning, she would get up and run and run and run—sometimes up to fourteen miles at a time. It was her only release from the pain of her sin. She was trying to outrun the consequences, the torturous memories, and the weight of her deceptive heart.

Paige's story was very different from Lisa's. She had been sexually molested as a child, developed a promiscuous lifestyle, became pregnant as a teen, and had an abortion. Yet when I talked to her I found she had a similar pattern of coping. In the early hours of the morning, when she could no longer cope with her feelings of guilt and anger and regret, she would get in her car and drive and drive and drive. Up and down the highway she would fly, craving the buzz and the energy of the night life to drown out the screaming in her soul. Anything but the quiet.

Lisa and Paige are extreme examples, but I've met many women whose way of coping with negative feelings was similar. The more I've talked to very busy women, in fact, the more I've come to realize that a jam-packed schedule is often just another form of running away from pain, from the truth about ourselves and our lives, and from the face of God.

No wonder we don't want to stop and rest. When we rest, letting our adrenaline levels drop and our minds slow down, it's easier to hear God speak. When He speaks, there is truth. And the truth He may choose to speak about a sinful condition or a wounded heart can be extremely painful.

No wonder we create a diversion and get ourselves busy once more. Whether it is the activity of exercising, working, or taking care of others, we let busyness overrun our lives. Busyness creates the buzz that dulls out the otherwise piercing voice of God. Like children plugging their ears to what they don't want to hear, we plug our lives with endless activities in an attempt to run out the time on the clock. We run from the truth of God and His whisperings about authentic living.

This is how my recently widowed friend Julie identified the busyness buffer in her life. She was drearily anticipating a week of alone time when her two children were away at camp. Under any other conditions, a mother might jealously hope for some quiet from all the activities of two children aged eight and ten, but in this case she was anxious with dread. Why? Because, as she honestly put it, she knew that once the kids were out of the house, she would have to face the awful truth about what had happened. She recognized that normally her children and all their activities helped her avoid the ugly reality of her husband's death and her feelings about it—especially her feelings about God. She put it this way: "I'm mad at God. I'm mad that He took the love of my life." Her form of running from these painful feelings was staying busy with her job and the kids' school schedule. But once the house was quiet, she knew she would have to address the hardest issues in her life—her aloneness and her anger at the apparent absence of God's compassion.

**Our hearts are noisy arenas. We have fightings within and fears without. (Wayne E. Oates)**

I don't know you, of course. I don't know if your busyness is a cover for negative feelings such as guilt, anger, sadness, or inadequacy. And I certainly can't say whether you're trying to close your ears to God. But I've seen it happen enough—even in my own life—that I have to raise the possibility. Do you have some truth to face? Is there something in your life that keeps you running harder and faster every year? If you feel driven by a schedule that seems to manage you instead of you managing it, could it be that you are allowing busyness to buffer you from facing some uncomfortable truth about your life or, more important, from hearing the voice of God?

There are many reasons we let busyness drive our schedules, and pain is only one of them. When a frantic pace takes over your life, you are probably trying to avoid something. Maybe it is an unresolved conflict with a parent or an abiding anger toward your spouse. Perhaps it is a sense of helplessness concerning a wayward child or despair over your lack of purpose or a failing sense of self-worth. Whatever the cause, the symptom can be the same—escaping into busyness.

The trouble, of course, is that the escape doesn't really work for long, and even when it accomplishes its purpose, it causes more problems. As you embrace a substitute for dealing with painful realities, you can actually busy yourself into a corner of internal isolation. Away from comfort. Away from growth. Away from God and His desire to help you live a life of rich meaning. And away from any hope of solving the problems that caused you to run in the first place.

Staying busy has become a national obsession. We pack our calendars with appointments and entertainments, with importance and ambition, with need-to-dos and want-to-dos. Most of us carry a full load, our days filled with endless scurrying. Busyness even becomes a badge of honor—we can't wait to tell somebody, *anybody*, how incredibly busy we are.

But have we paused to ask what the badge really means? What does all that crammed-schedule busyness signify? Busy means occupied, but by what?

Henry David Thoreau asked, "It is not enough to be busy. So are the ants. The question is: What are we busy about?" That is an excellent question. What are you busy about? Why are you so busy? Could it be that your busyness is taking you far away from God and His design for your life? Is all the busyness in your life really a form of running, of straying from God?

In Luke 15 we meet another person who ran away. He ran fast and far, determined to distance himself from family and familiarity. We don't know why he ran—perhaps to get away from his father's heavy expectations or his brother's angry self-righteousness or the responsibilities of home or his own internal anger or guilt. We do know that once he made his getaway, he spent his time and his money lavishly and foolishly. That's why he's called the prodigal—the one who was wasteful: "The younger son gathered all he had and took a journey into a far country, and there he squandered his property in reckless living" (v. 13). Jesus goes on to say that this prodigal young man didn't stop until "he had spent everything" (v. 14).

That's another thing that running does to your spirit. It creates a sense of being spent, breathless, worn-out, and depleted. Is there a chance you are spending your time lavishly and recklessly on things that are stealing your very life? Are you squandering your energy and time away from the presence of the very Father who desires to give you life?

I wonder . . . is running out the clock, racing from pain or relationships or a sense of worthlessness, creating a sense of utter exhaustion? Is it causing a lack of time for real life as you deeply desire it? If you allow the raging pace to overcome your life, you will find that your inner emptiness births a feeling of reckless living—a waste of life and a feeling of famine.

## Running From the Truth:
## The Trap of Toxic Busyness

God has so much more for you. You, like the prodigal son, can return to your Father and face the issues that stir your soul to dissatisfaction and create the need to run. He has promised to provide meaning in even the most despairing circumstances. He can calm your restless heart. He can balance your days. He wants to be the meaning in your life, the center of your schedule. And He can help you manage your schedule with healthy balance. He can help you love your life again.

**When I am constantly running there is no time for being. When there is no time for being there is no time for listening. (Madeleine L'Engle)**

God doesn't want us to squander our time on reckless living. He doesn't want us to run away from our problems or from Him. He's always ready to welcome us back home. We must simply be willing to find the way home.

Luke records that the prodigal son did just that. He came to his senses in a foreign land, realized what his running had done to himself and his family, and headed home.

*And he arose and came to his father. But while he was still a long way off, his father saw him and felt compassion, and ran and embraced him and kissed him. (v. 20)*

You know, that's the way God will embrace you once you find the courage to stop running. He will actually run to you if you acknowledge your need of His help. He not only feels compassion for you—He yearns for your return. So stop running and wasting time, and turn to Him. Move toward your loving heavenly Father who will supplant emptiness and pain with meaning and comfort, stability and love.

The road home is as simple as an acknowledgement that all the busyness in your life does not come close to supplying your needs the way God does. There is never anyone or anything that can calm and quiet your schedule or your soul the way God does.

Psalm 46:10 gives the Lord's words to us: "Be still, and know that

143

I am God." That's not always easy. It takes courage to back down from busyness and face the frightening emptiness behind it. It takes trust to listen for a Voice you're afraid to hear.

But the amazing thing about God is that He's not only waiting for you to be still—He's right there beside you, making it possible. Even as He waits for you to return, He is calling your name in love.

Right now, in this moment, try to be still and see that God is waiting for you, just like the prodigal's father, ready to open His arms and take you in.

Are you ready to come home?

## Time Out

• Identify some of the ways you tend to run from problems or have run from them in the past (excessive exercise, workaholism, excessive availability to people who need your help, shopping, overeating, etc.). What situations in your life tend to make these tendencies work?

• When could you establish some times of stillness and quietness in your day, some times to acknowledge God? If you find this difficult, try to identify why.

• What unhealthy patterns do you tend to use for coping with your pain?

• Tell a trusted friend about this pattern, and ask him or her to pray with you and for you. If necessary, talk with a counselor or minister.

# 18

# An Unseen Agenda:

## The Trap of Missing God's Appointments

"**The heart of man** plans his ways," says the book of Proverbs, "but the LORD establishes his steps" (16:9). I would have done well to remember that when my daughter Emily asked me to take her to her friend's house. You see, I was on my way out the door with some *very* important plans. I had an *appointment*.

My husband had given me a certificate to an oh-so-swanky spa in town. And I had finally managed to find time to go out to the spa, some thirty minutes away, and take advantage of the luxurious amenities. I had scheduled the appointment weeks in advance and was delirious with delight, imagining myself being pampered head to toe. Then my daughter Emily walked in to tell me she needed to be at Mary Martha's house by 4:30 that afternoon—on the *other* side of town, in the opposite direction of the spa.

I was incensed. Didn't Emily know I had an appointment? Hadn't I taken care of all the children's arrangements that day to insure that my swanky spa appointment would remain untouched? What in the world was she thinking—expecting me to take her to her friend's house right when I should be leaving for my little piece of spa heaven on earth?

After some serious mother hysteria (and an unwise decision to try and stuff it all in instead of telling Emily no), I told her to hurry up and get in the car. I thought I could manage to drop her off and rush back the opposite direction to the spa. As we sped away from the house, I warned her in my most serious tone that if there was one speck of traffic on the way to Mary Martha's, I would be turning the car around and taking her right back to our house. I did not have the time to sit in traffic because that would endanger my appointment.

I droned on mercilessly with platitudes about being on time, making plans in advance, and honoring commitments. I warned her about expecting me to drop *everything* and complete her plans. I would have continued, but with one look at the highway, I fell into silent seething. It was a parking lot. I slammed my hands on the steering wheel in a huff. I could feel my voice tensing up inside as I exclaimed, "I will *never* do this again!"

Emily sat silently—praying, I am sure, for a break in the traffic or for a break from the hysterics of her mother. By the time I finally got to Mary Martha's house, Emily was anxiously grabbing her bag and reaching for the door. I am sure she would have gladly jumped out of the moving car if she thought it might appease me. With a quick good-bye and some instructions for later, I screeched back down the highway toward the swanky spa.

Some twenty minutes down the road, I phoned home to check in with my husband. He mentioned that the swanky spa had called and left a message on our answering service. "What did they want?" I asked impatiently. He was unsure but offered to let me call in and check the message myself. Steering with one hand, balancing the cell phone in the other, I managed to dial into the message service.

"Mrs. Davis, this is Hilary at the 'Swanky Spa.' I am phoning to let you know that our nail tech had an emergency and needs to cancel your appointment. I am sorry for the late notice, as this is uncustomary for our fine facility, and we hope you will call back and schedule another appointment. Thank you, Mrs. Davis, and have a wonderful day!"

I was dumbfounded. There was no longer an appointment because it had been canceled, and without my knowledge. *Poof*—just like that it was gone. All my raving and speeding and unsafe cell phone usage— all for nothing.

## An Unseen Agenda:
## The Trap of Missing God's Appointments

That bizarre little situation made me begin to realize that I often let supposedly urgent appointments drive my life. The very things I think are so paramount are, in reality, nothing. Is getting to a spa appointment on time worth mistreating my daughter? Was my decision to try to cram it all in instead of calmly telling Emily I couldn't do it all worth it? In all my frantic hurry, was I missing my real appointment—which was whatever God had in mind for me that day?

**If someone were to ask me what is the most difficult lesson I've learned from [being paralyzed], I'm very clear about it: I know how to give when sometimes I really want to take. (Christopher Reeve)**

Here is a basic truth, but one I seem to have trouble getting into my head: God's agenda is not always the same as mine. God's schedule isn't the same as mine either. And when I get so caught up in my own plans that I forget to listen for God's guidance, that's usually when time stress gets the worst of me.

It's funny to me that we persist in thinking we own and manage our time with our little set of appointments. We work our schedules, imagining we navigate our purposes, persisting in the illusion that we are in charge.

But while we go about our day making scheduled appointments, some of which are prone to go *poof!* before our eyes, other kinds of appointments get grafted into our day of which we are largely unaware. They are the unscheduled appointments on our calendar, God-scheduled situations that arise in our lives. How we manage to handle them says everything about where our heart lies and speaks volumes about where God's heart lies.

One of the best unscheduled appointments in the Old Testament is the story of David. This son of Jesse was the youngest in a family full of brothers. He had been anointed king years before by the prophet Samuel. But at this point, other than the lingering remembrance of oil on his head, David had been given no other sign that he would take the throne. Instead he entered into the household of the current king, Saul, as a musician. In addition to his palace duties, he kept up with his home chores—tending the sheep. One day his father sent him to take provisions to his brothers, who were serving in the king's army. This set the stage for David to keep an otherwise invisible appointment.

The armies of Saul were facing off against the Philistines and their gargantuan warrior, Goliath. This champion giant had been taunting the Israelites, enticing them to fight, but none would take him on. So God moved in and provided David, a young man ready and willing to face a giant.

> David . . . came to the encampment as the host was going out to the battle line, shouting the war cry. And Israel and the Philistines drew up for battle, army against army. And David left the things in charge of the keeper of the baggage and ran to the ranks and went and greeted his brothers. As he talked with them, behold, the champion, the Philistine of Gath, Goliath by name, came up out of the ranks of the Philistines and spoke the same [taunting] words as before. And David heard him. (vv. 20-23)

Unbeknownst to David, he was on his way to an unscheduled, God-sized appointment that would live in Israelite history. David heard the giant, but he also heard his God, and he took on the appointment that the armies of Israel avoided.

**It helps to resign as the controller of your future. All that energy we expend to keep things running right is not what keeps things running right. (Anne Lamott)**

Can you imagine? Here came the little brother bringing in snacks of bread and cheese for the big boys. He heard a giant Philistine taunting "the armies of the living God" (v. 26), understood what was going on, and responded accordingly. Fighting Goliath was not penciled in anywhere in his day. Yet David could not stand to watch God's army lose courage with every word from the giant. So he took what he had and killed the Philistine while all of Israel watched.

Had he anticipated this moment of glory when he walked toward the lines with the bread basket? Of course not, just as he had not antic-ipated becoming a musician for Saul. But in his heart David held his schedule open for what God had in mind. You see, it was only by accepting the providence of being an errand boy for his brothers that he was able to kill the giant who had otherwise been undefeated. David remained open to God's appointments for his life so that when the unscheduled opportunity popped up, he was literally ready for action.

I realize you and I are not necessarily on a vocational track to become a queen or king. However, we *are* on a kingdom track for God, and there are no coincidences where God is concerned. Therefore, we must be ready for action, maintaining a kingdom mind-set where our appointments are concerned, even the unscheduled ones.

What is a kingdom mind-set? It's basically a matter of keeping God's agenda in mind. And the guiding principle of God's agenda is always love.

Jesus made this very clear when He was asked to identify the most important of God's commandments. His answer was simple:

> *"The most important is, 'Hear, O Israel: The Lord our God, the Lord is one. And you shall love the Lord your God with all your heart and with all your soul and with all your mind and with all your strength.' The sec-ond is this: 'You shall love your neighbor as yourself.' There is no other commandment greater than these." (Mark 12:29-31)*

Loving God and loving people—according to Jesus, there is no greater calling. And the two are intertwined: there is no real love for God without love for people as well. It is the benchmark of the believer to love and care for others, to make other people our urgent priority, to base all our scheduling decisions on the guiding principle of love.

In the case of my spa fiasco, the problem was not really my appoint-ment. I actually think I had a right to that appointment and even a responsibility to keep it. In fact, I believe that keeping scheduled appointments can be a way of honoring and loving others. But in all honesty, that wasn't my motivation that morning.

I also believe I had a perfect right to tell Emily I couldn't take her to her friend's house because of my appointment. I could have done that in a loving way. But I didn't. Instead I let my stress over the appointment determine how I would treat my daughter. I ranted and raved instead of treating her with love and respect. I put my hurry over her humanity. And for that I had to seek both her forgiveness and God's.

Jesus never looked into a set of eyes without appreciating that person's importance to God. The people in our life are not scheduling problems; in fact, they should become our scheduling priorities. I believe God wants us to treat our schedules with an open hand, looking for opportunities to surrender our personal plans in order to love our neighbor.

If I had not made so much of my swanky spa appointment, I seriously doubt I would have treated Emily so unkindly. My own needs became my priority. And God knew I needed the appointment to fall apart before my eyes so I could appropriately evaluate my intentions. Perhaps that is why Jesus warns us to love God with *all our strength*. Sometimes that is what it takes to keep our values right.

How often do you remember to think of the goings on in your life—the *people* in your life—as appointments with God? With a little stretch of imagination and a whole lot of patience, you might begin to start to see that God is always about the business of making His business your business.

And God's business, minute by minute, is always and eternally about love.

## Time Out

• Describe an appointment in your own life that went *poof!* What was your immediate emotional reaction?

• Why is it important to keep appointments when possible and not create a *poof!* in someone else's day?

• How likely are you to be like David and move forward to unscheduled but all-important appointments?

• Above all else, God asks that we love one another. How is your schedule directly related to loving other people?

## PART FOUR

# The Time of Your Life:

## Clearing the Way for Joy

When I walked into my son's room two days before he was to leave for college, I knew we were in for a little work. The floor was practically hidden by old, crumpled school papers, recently opened graduation gifts lying here and there, piles of clothes (clean and dirty), and a big black duffle bag filled with who knows what in the middle of everything.

I had been asking Will for weeks about the packing plan. And for weeks he had assured me there was no need for a plan because he could handle it all in just a few days. No doubt he could. But it would certainly require a lot of concentrated energy in a short amount of time. We were less than forty-eight hours away from moving him to a new city to embark on a new challenge. But before he could embark on his new and exciting life, my Will had some work to do—some papers to trash and some clothes to clean and some bags to pack.

It is one thing to have an impulse to change your life for the better. Actually doing it is something else entirely. Clearing the path for joy is about doing the necessary next thing, even if it's sometimes laborious, so that you can get to the new and exciting way of living.

Reading this book and even agreeing with it in principle will do little to move you down the road to more joyful living. The real changes come when you start applying God's truth to your life, asking Him for the insight and energy needed to start accomplishing all that comes with gained wisdom.

You might realize you have some things to clear out of your way on this path to balance and rest in your schedule. Making a plan and implementing change could just be the thing to get you on the road to abundant living in your daily life.

Seize this time by planning for the journey ahead . . . and clear the path for joy!

# 19

# Do the Math:

## Getting Real About Your Schedule

**Lots of things about life** are unfair and unpredictable, but time isn't one of them. Every day you are alive, you wake up with the same amount of time. And every human being gets exactly the same amount as you do.

I think it's very considerate of God to handle time in such a fashion. Can you even imagine what life would be like if we all had differing amounts? Time covetousness would abound. And how insecure would you feel if you never knew how much time you would receive for a given day? But God didn't do things that way. He chose to distribute this gift with absolute equality and complete dependability. We all get the same time allowance, and we receive it predictably—the same amount every day.

What varies, of course, is the way we spend our time. And it is in the spending that some issues surface.

Some people truly seem have all the time in the world. They ease through life serenely, doing what they think is most important, calmly letting go of the rest.

Other people—like most of the people I know—seem chronically short of time. They're always running late, always coming up short, forever frantic, constantly in a hurry, busy to the point of panic.

## The Time of Your Life

All too often, despite my best intentions, my life has been like that. And so, most likely, has yours.

For example, you know that you only have so much time. You also know that how you spend that time reflects your priorities or your values. Now, hopefully you are living a life within the framework of choosing what is important to fit the available time. But what if all that is true and you still feel frantic and busy?

I know I have experienced that very problem in my life. The more I thought about it, the more curious I became to understand what was going on with my feelings of busyness and lack of time. So I tried an experiment.

I realized that there are only so many hours in my day and that I had only so much available energy to do what I needed to do. And I was curious to know if my priorities were being reflected accurately in how I chose to spend my days.

I needed to look into where I was spending my time allowance. So I sat down one Saturday morning, thought back over my week, and made a chart. I got a legal pad and, starting on the left-hand side of the paper, listed my waking hours in thirty-minute segments. Then I went back in and filled in what I was doing with my time during those segments.

Next, I grouped all my various activities into categories—carpooling, errand running, office work, housework, yard work, recreational time, date time (with my husband), church activities, volunteering, time spent with friends, time spent reading, prayer time, TV time, computer time, exercise, and so on. That way I could see how many hours a week I spent on each type of activity.

**The daily pressures to act, to do, to decide, make it difficult to stop and think, to consider, and to examine your life goals, directions, and priorities—to find the best choices you have for managing your own world. (Roy Menninger)**

Over the course of the next week and weekend (when I spend my time differently), I checked my chart periodically to make sure that I hadn't missed anything as far as my time expenditure was concerned. After the week was over, I totaled up my categories again and analyzed the chart with my priorities in mind. This enabled me to look at my life accurately and see where my time was going.

What an eye-opener!

I quickly discovered that the reality of how I actually spent my days did not accurately reflect my dreamy view of my life priorities. I had actually suspected that. But as I looked closer, I realized I had a more basic problem: bad math. I was planning my schedule as though I had more hours in my week than I actually had.

The truth is that most Americans live with this kind of bad math when it comes to their time. This is a form of denial. We schedule ourselves into oblivion without ever facing the fact that our allotted daily twenty-four hours will come nowhere close to accommodating all our plans and desires. Then when the inevitable happens, when we run out of time—perhaps for something we care about most—we're surprised and stressed.

You'd think it would be fairly simple to not schedule more for yourself than your time will allow. However, the abundance of time management books and programs on the market testifies to the fact that we just can't get this through our heads.

When I filled out my time chart, I was most shocked to see that one of my main priorities, my husband, was not reflected adequately in my week. During my busy days, that was the one relationship that became expendable. After realizing this, I talked with Will, and together we decided to make that priority real in my (and his) schedule.

I also was disappointed that I spent so much time "keeping house." Though I love homekeeping, I felt that routine chores were taking up time I'd rather spend on priorities I value more. (I would truly rather spend time with my husband or children than dust my trinkets or vacuum.) Once I saw what I was doing, I realized I had several choices:

I could resign myself to the reality of spending $x$ number of hours a week dusting, cleaning, and the like. (My priorities wouldn't let me do this.)

I could live with a dustier house. (I could relax a little this way, but not much.)

I could hire someone to help me. (This was a possibility if I could manage it financially).

Or I could simplify my housekeeping chores by downsizing, getting rid of many of the objects I spent so much time maintaining. (Bingo. This I could do.)

Now I had a plan for action. I cleared the house of all the extraneous clutter, and we had (as my husband refers to it) "the mother of all garage sales." The items that were more valuable (but no longer valued) I shuttled to a local consignment store. I spent some of the money I made from selling the extra stuff—it was more than I expected!—to hire someone to help me clean my home. And after having that help for a while, I realized it was a value to me to build it into our budget. Then I made sure I invested the time I saved (by having help) in activities that matter more to me than housecleaning. I also carefully noted the fact that whenever I went out shopping I was adding to an already full closet and an overloaded house. Now I try to keep in mind that every material purchase comes with a surtax of maintenance and energy . . . and time.

For me, the result of my basic math exercise has been a noticeable improvement in the quality of my family's life together. In fact, I have even decided it's a good idea to repeat the exercise every three months or so during this very crucial time in my family's life. I have children at home. My son just graduated from high school and started college. My two girls are starting new school years. This is a season not to be missed. I do not want to look back with regret because I was too busy dusting—or deceived by my bad math. I'm learning that just as checking the balance of a bank account is a necessary evil, so is checking the balance of a schedule. A regular inventory can keep you out of trouble.

My time inventory highlighted another "math issue" for me that I think is true for many other people as well: we forget to allow extra time for emergencies or even those inevitable little delays. We pack our schedules and our children's schedules without a thought for even a traffic tangle on the way to soccer practice.

I can't believe I do this. Denying the possibility of traffic issues in a town the size of Austin is just plain silly. So is planning as if there will never be an emergency, an accident, or an unforeseen development. But

I do tend to plan that way. And then I'm frustrated when I run behind in my schedule.

My husband, actually, has even more difficulty than I do in this regard. I'm always amused when he calls from his office at the church and tells me he'll be home for dinner in ten minutes. I immediately triple that estimate because I know some things about my husband. For one thing, Will is friendly. He will not leave the office without saying good-bye to his fellow workers. Second, there will be sluggish traffic at rush hour when he starts his commute home. It is practically impossible for him to get home and sit down to dinner in ten minutes. And I learned that the hard way, believing my husband's "bad math" and watching many dinners grow cold on the table. The estimates he gave me were just plain unrealistic, and his believing he could meet them did not change the basic math facts.

It is always easier to see this tendency in someone else's life, however—and much harder to spot it in your own. Sometimes, no matter how carefully you track your hours and plan your days, you can't get a handle on what's going wrong with your schedule. You can check and recheck your math and just not be able to see your mistake—often because of something intangible and unforeseen.

That happened to me about three months into my new job, when I began to suspect that something was seriously wrong with my schedule—or wrong with *me*. I would be fruitful and capable from the early-morning hours until about 5 in the afternoon. But after that, on many evenings, I would come apart, caving into exhausted tears after dinner. During the time when Will and I usually caught each other up on the day, I could barely keep my eyes open.

I couldn't figure out what was wrong with me. I was definitely feeling overloaded, but when I looked at my schedule I didn't see why. I hadn't added *that* many hours to my day. In fact, I had done the math carefully, planning so I could fit everything in. All my activities seemed to jigsaw together beautifully. And yet I still felt like I had more than I could handle. I knew something had to change. The hard part was figuring out what. Should I quit my part-time job? Discontinue working out? Stop writing? Blow off involvement at church? Quit horseback riding? Get counseling? What was it?

# The Time of Your Life

While reading my Bible early one Tuesday morning, I found the beginning of the answer in Hebrews 4:12-13:

*For the word of God is living and active. Sharper than any double-edged sword, it penetrates even to dividing soul and spirit, joints and marrow; it judges the thoughts and attitudes of the heart. Nothing in all creation is hidden from God's sight. Everything is uncovered and laid bare before the eyes of him to whom we must give account.* (NIV)

I suddenly realized that only God understands the full reality of what is really going on in my life, my time included. He penetrates my thoughts and attitudes. He uncovers my motives. And His math is far better than mine.

For me at that moment of my life, it was clear that I needed to rely on God for the answer. "Expose my real need," I begged God. "Do an exposé on my life." I wanted Him to reveal what my problem was so I could act on my real need issues, not my perceived issues. "Whatever it takes," I prayed.

### I am learning that there is always time for the things the Lord wants us to do. (Karen Mains)

Well, it didn't take long for God to answer my prayer, though not in the gentle fashion I had expected. I had decided to go into work early that morning so I could leave early for a doctor's appointment. (Did I mention that my new schedule left no extra room for extras such as appointments? Not too smart.) At any rate, as I sat down to the computer and started answering e-mails, our office manager walked in and barked, "What are you doing here? You're not supposed to be here."

I looked up and burst into tears. The office manager looked baffled. We sat down and talked. And that was the breakthrough I needed.

To make a long story short, she too had been at the short end of her stick that morning. She had spoken too sharply, and I had been overly sensitive. We both apologized. But I also came away from that conversation with a much clearer understanding of why I was so on edge with my schedule.

## Do the Math:
## Getting Real About Your Schedule

Part of the problem, of course, was that I had packed my schedule too tightly, not leaving room in it for emergencies or situations such as doctor appointments. But something else was involved as well, something that had tilted my scheduling math in an unpredictable direction. Although my calculations had been fairly accurate in regard to actual hours and minutes—work time, commute time, family time, and so on—I had failed to count the cost of such intangibles as emotion and energy.

With the new job, the hours, and the paycheck came the pressure of new intangible responsibilities, new relationships, new personal goals, fresh creative ideas, and a framework of professional evaluation—and these new elements in my life, though welcome, came with an energy price tag. That is, I had less energy to spend in the time allotted because part of my energy was being spent to process all those changes.

What could I do? Well, I couldn't do anything about processing the changes—that just went with the territory of my life. Neither could I squeeze more hours into my day. So the only thing left to do was to recalculate my schedule and do some subtraction. Good-bye to book club and hello one more evening a month at home with the family. Good-bye to elaborate entertaining and hello to some relaxed standards for what a "clean" house really looks like.

Best of all, hello to a regained sense of balance.

I'm still trying some things to see if I feel relieved of the pressures, and I'm still watching for God's exposé to reveal new things about my life. I'm trying to focus on the truly important elements in my life and regularly skim off the surface items that won't be missed in the long run. But I am finding that making the right choices, though difficult, helps energize my life—and that energy in turn makes it easier to maintain a positive attitude.

It's basic math, but there's still more to it than meets the eye. Sure, it's hours and minutes, but it's something else too.

By God's calculation, my honesty plus God's truth equals more energy for every hour of my day—and lots more joy for the rest of my life.

## Time Out

• What would you list as the top five priorities in your life? Looking at the big picture and at what you want most from life, what five elements are truly most important to you? Make a list, fold it up, and put it away for a while.

• Try setting up a time chart like the one I describe in this chapter. Fill out your chart over the course of a week or two, recording the time you spend on various kinds of activities. Try to record what you do on a fairly regular basis. You may be tempted at this point to alter your schedule as you go in order to reflect your priorities better, but try not to do that at this point.

• After setting up your time chart, pull out the five-priorities list and see how well your actual time expenditures match up with your most important priorities.

• What important realistic demands of life do you tend to forget or deny when you're planning your schedule? What kinds of intangibles such as emotion and energy drain do you typically forget to plan for?

• How does bringing the energy issue into the equation change the way you look at your calendar math? Can you think of ways that actually *adding* activities (prayer, Bible study, exercise, personally fulfilling activities) could help ease your schedule woes by adding more energy to your life?

# 20

# Saying N-O:

## The Negative Path to Positive Joy

**What is it about** the little word *no* that creates such problems for us women? I have talked with more friends and colleagues than I care to relate about the issues associated with the little word *no*. Saying it must make women feel very unpopular and stigmatized, because there's a mile-long line of people I know who are living in regret because they didn't say no about something.

We agree to be on committees we don't have time for, we drive carpools we have no business being in, do favors we just don't have time to do, and we lead Bible studies we never even meant to attend. We agree to commitments we don't want to make and activities we'd enjoy but just can't spare the time for. We hand over the reins of our lives to other people and then end up angry or resentful—all because we have trouble saying that terrifying little two-letter word.

It's not that we don't know how to pronounce it. It's that we have trouble understanding when we should say it . . . and difficulty saying it forcefully enough that other people will pay attention. (Sometimes we even have trouble telling ourselves no.)

I have made my share of mistakes in this regard. I'll never forget being in our first home, newly married, with my husband pastoring his first church. I had made a new friend at church who had a lot of great ideas for my life—most of them based on the activities of my immediate predecessor in her life. On and on she went about how fabulous her previous pastor's wife had been, how hospitable, and how spiritual. Why, that amazing woman had even hosted a buffet supper at her house for the entire church! You know what's coming next, right? Before I knew it, I was entertaining the congregation at my new home. (I did offer a dessert buffet instead of a supper buffet!)

I can tell you that I was a wreck in the weeks before that event. I had never wanted the entire church tromping through my house. I dreaded the invasion of privacy. I had no extra time to enjoy planning a party of this magnitude. I was managing my two-year-old, my school schedule (I was trying to finish college at a university some sixty miles away), my new house, our new church . . . and now "my" dessert buffet.

By God's grace, I got through it all, determined never to repeat the mistake. And I did learn something important from the ordeal. I learned that I should never let myself be driven by someone else's priority. My friend should have hosted the buffet since it was something she really cared about. She would have been great at it. It belonged in *her* schedule, not mine.

At the same time, I can't really say that woman was the only person at fault in that situation. Perhaps she could have been less pushy, but the decision to say no to that buffet was my responsibility.

Back then I just couldn't do it. I hope I could do it today.

But why is saying no so difficult? We've already looked at a number of possible reasons. Bad math, as we saw in the previous chapter, can be a factor—we say yes to too much because we don't accurately assess the limits of our time and energy. This is often the case when we say yes to opportunities that appeal to us but don't really fit our schedule.

**Most of us are tempted to respond immediately to requests. We're almost programmed that way— and our first instinct is to say yes. We're flattered to be asked. We like the feeling of being needed. And we're willing to overlook the important difference between being asked and being called. I've found I**

## Saying N-O:
## The Negative Path to Positive Joy

**can short-circuit this process if I can delay my yes long enough to seriously seek God's direction. (Alice Gray and Steve Stephens)**

Confusion about our priorities and difficulty in making decisions are other reasons why it can be hard to say no. We may say yes inappropriately because we haven't taken the time to honestly assess what is most important to us and how we want to focus our energies. We may have an immature fear of limiting our options and need to grow up a little.

For most women, however, an inability to say no has more to do with our self-esteem—or a lack of it. It's related to our people-pleasing tendencies. We hunger for approval, to be liked; so we say yes and think it won't matter that much if we add just one more little thing to our schedule—one more little meeting or whatever. Over and over we say yes in order to get the pat on the back, to be known as the dependable one, the loyal one, the one to call for help. But sometimes we're the ones who need the help. We need the strength and the confidence to assess our priorities, make our decisions, and speak up for ourselves.

Where can we find that confidence? For me, it comes from understanding the resources God has made available to us.

Within the boundaries of His law, God has given each of us a lot of freedom (and responsibility) for decision-making. He has entrusted us with our lives—an awesome responsibility when you think of it. He has also given us His Word and the Holy Spirit and the counsel of others for guidance and support. We also have His assurance that we are loved and cherished, that He gave His only Son to redeem us, and that we each have a unique calling on this earth. We each have the necessary equipment to hear from God about the issues in our lives and to act on his calling. And the ability to say no is an essential part of that equipment.

Jesus Himself sometimes answered no, even with those He loved the most. He gave a no to Martha and Mary when Lazarus was sick, declining to visit until His friend had died—all for the higher purpose of God's glory. He often gave a no to the crowds when He was tired or needed to spend time with His Father. He gave a no to the disciples more times than I care to count—teaching them by word and example how to live. He was able to stay no when necessary because He fully understood His purpose. He derived energy and strength—and the discernment to say no—from understanding why He was here on earth—and why He wasn't.

Jesus' boundaries were based firmly on His purposes, and He was confident, even vehement in protecting them. Remember when Peter pulled Him aside to let Him know that He needed to protect His image and stop talking about dying? The Lord's answer in Matthew 16:23 was blistering: "Get behind me, Satan!" He said. "You are a stumbling block to me; you do not have in mind the things of God, but the things of men" (NIV).

Those are stinging words. I wouldn't necessarily recommend using them for turning down the chairman of the PTA or the neighborhood association. But couldn't you use some of that same forcefulness and energy to protect your own priorities—to focus your energy on your true passions and your appropriate life mission?

I'm not saying you should be rude or hostile or that you should always go it alone. Certainly it is wise to seek counsel in your decisions, to honor the opinions of others. But it is even wiser to develop a pattern of turning to God for your final answers—and for strength and self-confidence to say no when it's appropriate.

I told a friend yesterday that she needed to say no in her life. She's a wife and a mother of three who works a part-time job at her kids' school. She loves the work. The only problem is that it's a twenty-hour-a-week job, and she spends forty to fifty hours a week doing it. My friend cried as she complained that the job had outgrown her initial expectation, her boss depends on her for leadership, and she has doubled the people she is in charge of managing.

I certainly understand how that could happen. But I gently suggested that she needed either to work the twenty hours she agreed to and let the pieces fall where they may or discuss the option of full-time work with her employer.

**Remember that recreation and relaxation are *necessities,* not extras. And then concentrate on identifying those activities and commitments in**

**your life that have been imposed by others, that just don't fit your life plan, and that bring your life no joy and meaning. (Charles Bradshaw and Dave Gilbert)**

The truth is, as long as my friend is willing to work fifty hours at a part-time job, she will remain in her predicament. She's making a choice by not saying no—and that choice is to say yes, yes, yes. Every time she packs up her work to take it home, every time she hides in her bedroom and works while her kids and husband are downstairs spending family time together, every time she comes into the office when she's not supposed to be there, she's saying yes to someone else's priorities and is ignoring the specific call of God on her own life.

It doesn't make sense, does it? In fact, it's a little bit insane—like something I did at my last horse show.

You need to understand that I'm not a professional horse handler. Riding for me is a hobby and a passion as well as a form of exercise. I dearly love spending time at the barn and taking lessons and even trying my hand in amateur hunter-jumper competitions. But I do it for fun—and I'm far from an expert—as you will see.

On this particular day I was on a beautiful, capable animal and was making my round in a local hunter-jumper show, competing against others of my ability level. Each of us was expected to take our horse over some eight to ten jumps in specific sequence. As with a piano recital, there was a judge and an audience.

I was cantering the mare down a four-stride line with two jumps. But as I went over the first jump in the line I lost my balanced position on the horse's back. I still had my feet in the stirrups, but I was flying like Superman over the saddle, my body parallel to the horse's back. Experienced riders would agree that this is not a sound position to take on a horse at any time, especially not in a horse show.

I tried to maintain my dignity and reestablish my seat in the next several strides before the second jump came up. The problem was that my unbalanced position and the horse's motion over the jump threw me at the horse's neck, so I held on for dear life. That is called neck riding, and it is a definite no-no in the show ring.

Now I was really in trouble. The horse was cantering along toward the upcoming jump, and I was wrapped around her neck, moving along in rhythm. From under my helmet, I could see that the jump was seconds in front of me. It was clearly time to pull her up and stop the ride, which was ruined anyway. But somehow, irrationally, I thought I could pull it off, that there was a chance I could either get back up on the saddle or just take the jump while clinging to the mare's neck. So instead of reining my horse in, I just held on and hoped for the best.

Lucky for me, the horse had more sense than I did. She stopped bolt upright in front of the jump, and I flew full force into it. Needless to say, there was a huge crash and a series of gasps from the audience. Unhurt but mortified, I got up, brushed the sand from my breeches, and told her, "I'm so sorry." I couldn't believe I'd been stupid enough to try that jump.

*Yes, yes, yes*, I had said, *I can do this*, when the truth of the matter was there was no way I could do it. I had risked my very life flying toward that jump on that animal. Insane. Who did I think I was?

Which of course brings up yet another reason we sometimes have trouble saying no. Pride can often play a role in making "insane" decisions about our lives. We just won't say no because we want to save face with the people we respect. We have a strong need to be perceived in a certain light. Of course, that's about as stupid as my concerning myself with how the judge felt about me crashing into the jump. I'm sure she wasn't impressed. But what the judge felt about me was beside the point. I was about to kill myself.

Are you killing yourself on behalf of someone else's priorities, saying yes to activities and commitments you have no business pursuing? It's time to break free and lean on God as you make decisions about your schedule, to ask Him for the strength and confidence to make saying no a regular part of your week. If you need to, practice saying the words so they'll be easier to get out.

Remember, someone's asking you to do something does not necessarily make it God's will for your life. Neither does having the ability to do something or even the desire to do it. I urge you to get some listening ears and hear what God has to say about your self-worth, your priorities, and your decision-making.

## Saying N-O:
## The Negative Path to Positive Joy

If you are flying around at breakneck speed, risking the things that are most precious to you because you can't say no, Titus 2:4 has a wise word for you. That verse is primarily about mentoring—urging older women to teach younger women. But it wants them to teach young and old women alike to be "sane and sober of mind (temperate, disciplined) and to love their husbands and their children" (AMP).

The word no, in many instances, is a battle cry of the sane and the sober. It's a trademark of wisdom and maturity, the favorite tool of those who really want to protect what they love the most.

It's such a powerful little word: n-o.

With God's help, you can pronounce it today and thus say yes to balance, wisdom, and joy.

# Time Out

• Why is saying no sometimes the absolutely nicest thing you can say to someone in regard to your time?

• What circumstances make it especially difficult for you to say no to other people's priorities?

• What kind of insanity is created for you and your family when you give a yes when you should give a no?

• Talk with a spiritual friend who can help you get to the key issues associated with your difficulty in saying no in your life. Ask her for help in learning how to do this when necessary.

• During a quiet moment, sit down and write a list of no answers you could give to a request that isn't congruent with your priorities. "No, I can't manage that right now." "No, I've put a moratorium on new activities." "No, my schedule is full." Or simply, "Sorry . . . no." Actually practice saying these phrases out loud so they will come more easily when needed. You don't have to be rude, but practice being direct and speaking with finality. Try not to be hesitant or let your voice go up at the end like a question.

# 21

# Saying Y-E-S:

## What God Can Do with an Open Heart

**The afternoon is singing spring.** And my husband just walked out the door, taking the girls to my parents' ranch, with the words on his lips, "I don't want to be remembered as the dad who always said no."

We're a week out from Easter, which is easily the biggest Sunday of the year for my pastor husband. He could easily spend all day studying for next weekend—and probably feels the need to. But his priority today is family—specifically, two little girls who will not fully understand now but in time will remember a man who was committed to be a yes in their lives. A yes to going to the ranch, a yes to playing Battleship on a Friday night, a yes to making pancakes on a Saturday morning, and a yes to pulling them behind the boat on an inner tube.

Y-e-s is an even more powerful word than n-o. In fact, it's the *reason* we need to learn to say no—rejecting others' priorities so we can say a powerful yes to our own. Rejecting the things that aren't part of God's call so we can open our hearts to what is.

Last week I attended a funeral; the father of a childhood friend had died. I didn't know him well, but that funeral made me realize my friend was blessed to be raised by such a man. Every person who eulogized him said essentially the same thing: "He was a giver." And they weren't talking about money but time—exactly what my husband was giving to our girls.

# The Time of Your Life

All this made me wonder: How will I be remembered after I'm gone? If it were all to end for me today, what would people say?

I'm sure my recent experiences have predisposed me to think that way because not long ago I had a close call. I was on my way to the barn at 8:30 on a damp morning. A dense mist had coated the streets. I had barely begun my morning trek down a twisted stretch of road called FM 2222 when I spotted an oversized work van barreling straight toward me at fifty miles an hour. I remember fleeting thoughts: *He's drunk . . . He's lost control . . . He's going to hit me . . . Brake . . . Turn out . . . I might die.* And then I heard an indescribable sound. The impact sent my car spinning into the center stripe. I smelled something burning before I saw anything. But all I could think was, *I'm still alive.* I gently and searchingly touched my face, feeling for blood. I exhaled, struggling to get out of the car. As soon as I felt my legs moving, I realized I had another chance. Another chance to speak with my husband, another chance to hug my children, another chance to tell my parents I love them, and another chance to cling tightly to God. Another chance to say a resounding yes to fulfilling God's desires in my life.

In the movie *Hope Floats* one of the characters warns, "It's the worst kind of extravagance, to spend all your chances as if there is another one waiting around the corner." I fear our culture tends to breed that kind of extravagance. Our relative wealth and security—even now, with all our problems, America is still the land of plenty—tends to leave us careless about the need to make everlasting decisions.

But occasionally situations surface that prompt us to fight for spiritual focus. They surge up and demand attention, just as my wreck did. Sometimes they scream and cry like an inconsolable baby, grinding our schedules to a halt. And they are blessings of enormous magnitude, if we let them, allowing us to refocus on what God really wants for our lives.

**"That man," said the little prince to himself, ". . . is the only one of them all who does not seem to me ridiculous. Perhaps that is because he is thinking of something else besides himself." (Antoine de Saint-Exupery)**

## Saying Y-E-S:
## What God Can Do with an Open Heart

Even Old Testament prophets needed to be reminded of God's schedule. Isaiah found his life a wreck in the year that King Uzziah died. In a moment of despair over the future and leadership of his nation, he searchingly looked to God for relief. God answered his questions with a question of His own. And peering into God's blueprint for his life, Isaiah took hold of his own readiness.

*And I heard the voice of the Lord, saying, "Whom shall I send, and who will go for us?" Then I said I, "Here am I! Send me." (Isaiah 6:8)*

"Here am I! Send me"—that's just another form of yes. How different would our world be if God had His hands full of Christians ready to say yes. When the important assignments surge to the surface, we would then be guardians of God's predestined—although often surprising—purposes.

God's assignments tend to come when we least expect them, and in forms we may not be looking for. When the car breaks down or the kids get sick, at the longest line in the grocery store or with the shortest-tempered teacher at school, God may have something in mind for you. And no matter what the appointment brings, at every turn, could you cheerfully give a yes?

Imagine how life could change for you and for me if we would begin to treat every moment with assurance of divine appointment. No struggling. No striving. Just "Here am I. Yes. Here am I."

That happened to me recently at a local grocery/café known as Central Market.

I hadn't planned on seeing anyone the evening Will and I escaped there to have a quick dinner date. I had spent the majority of the day at the barn riding, and my appearance spoke loudly of the fact. I had debated getting dressed up, but Will made a point of assuring me that he didn't mind a date with a girl in boots and jeans, no matter how unkempt. I honestly thought we could sneak in and out, clandestine fashion, without having to see anyone we knew. I had planned it that way.

When we walked up to the café and I saw the line extending out the door, I glanced at Will in annoyance. This was not what I had expected on an early Thursday evening. There were people everywhere. I was somewhat self-conscious about the obvious lack of care I had taken in getting ready and hoped all the more to avoid seeing anyone we knew.

Well, it didn't take long before a man Will and I knew walked up and started a conversation. He went to our church and was happy to converse with us about the church and life. At that point I realized I had lost the anonymity I sought. So I smiled to myself and decided to let go. "OK, God. So I need to expect to see people in public and be ready to be nice even when I'm in my barn clothes."

Almost before the prayer was finished, a tall woman whom I recognized but did not know by name approached me. "Hi, Susie. I'm so glad to see you because I was wondering about the church retreat you're teaching at in two weeks. I am trying to decide whether to go."

Well, I had just promised to be nice. So I smiled and engaged in conversation, encouraging the woman to go to the retreat. But I didn't really understand the purpose of that divine appointment until two weekends later, when I found myself counseling that woman about some tough spiritual issues. Apparently our conversation in Central Market had helped her feel comfortable with me. She opened up to me about her struggles, shared silent agonies, and wept. We both cried as we prayed together. I had the distinct sense that something eternal happened in that time together.

It was a powerful moment, a holy moment. And it had its inception that night at Central Market when I said yes to God. Although Will and I enjoyed a dinner date, I'm convinced that was not the primary reason we went. The real reason was the encounter I hadn't anticipated with a woman who needed my love and care.

How many times do you find yourself in those curious situations—one of those invisible God-assigned appointments we talked about in a previous chapter? The truth is, often they feel like interruptions. Do you ever feel irritated by such encounters? Are you anxious to get away and get on with your life? Are you tired by the constant demands on your time?

You're not alone. Did you know even Jesus felt tired by human engagement, that He desired some anonymity? How did He handle the inevitable wrecked schedule? How did He keep on saying yes to the surprising, unscheduled appointments?

In John 4 we find Jesus "wearied . . . from his journey" (v. 6) and sitting beside a well. Enter a woman from Samaria—the unscheduled appointment from the Father. Jesus, tired though He was, took the time to talk with that woman. He made her a priority. And here's the interesting thing to note: Upon that woman's departure, Jesus was energized. He was fueled by completing the appointment set before Him. He told His disciples, "My food is to do the will of him who sent me and to accomplish his work" (v. 34). Had Jesus avoided the Samaritan woman, would He have found the same refreshment?

Responding to peevish (or pleasant) people encounters are what the food of God is about for the believer. The phone calls, the grocery store run-ins, the carpool lines and coffee stops—all carry the possibilities of the divine. All along the way, all throughout the day, God is making important people appointments for us. He has the calendar out, penciling in people throughout the day. He wants your availability. And He wants to refresh you through these encounters, just as He refreshed me through my encounter. Like the kind of refreshment I received when I was open to the meeting with the woman at Central Market. Though I went in for food and drink and a dinner date with Will, I left remembering that God is all about using me along the way to nourish others. And by doing so, He pours deeply into me as well, nourishing my soul by "accomplishing his work."

If indeed we are able to remember Christ's command to love our neighbor as ourselves, we must commit to being willing to spend our time on people.

C. S. Lewis states it dramatically in *The Weight of Glory*: "There are no ordinary people. You have never talked to a mere mortal." Lewis reminds us that "next to the Blessed Sacrament itself, your neighbor is the holiest object presented to your senses. If he is your Christian neighbor, he is holy in almost the same way, for in him also Christ *vere latitat*—the glorifier and the glorified, Glory Himself, is truly hidden." Therefore He exhorts us to think often of others' problems rather than just our own. He claims it is impossible to "think too often or too deeply about that of his neighbor. The load, or weight, or burden of my neighbor's glory should be laid on my back, a load so heavy that only humility can carry it, and the backs of the proud will be broken."[1]

I love and hate the fact that Lewis places my neighbor squarely on my shoulders. There are days when I feel full of Christ, able to hold the weight. Then there are days when I wish with all my heart that people would just go away. It takes a real effort of my will and imagination to remember that I can only carry the weight in the first place because God carries it with me—and that He will provide me with the strength and energy I need to do what He calls me to do. In the end, it is not my obedience that wears me down, but my disobedience.

The truth is, we always can expect the unexpected in life. There will always be someone who pops up in our days and needs a few moments of encouragement and time. We're wise, therefore, to plan with people in mind.

What does this mean in practical terms? It means roping off time for the people who are a regular part of our lives, as my husband roped off time for our two girls.

It also means leaving a little air in our schedules so we can respond to divine appointments without toppling the entire day's plan. Even building in an extra fifteen minutes while running errands could make a huge difference to someone you just might meet along the way.

**Twenty years from now you will be more disappointed by the things that you didn't do than by the ones you did do. (Mark Twain)**

And it's always wise to schedule in time for rest so that we have the energy to respond to whoever God sends our way—family, neighbors, or strangers. Jesus certainly did this. One reason He was able to meet the ongoing demands of helping people was that He understood the need to fuel Himself with time away from people. By doing the same for ourselves, we effectively make time for others.

And this of course brings us to the paradox of yes and no, the truth that saying yes to people may involve saying no to people as well. Saying yes to God's agenda in my life may well mean I say no to one person's request in order to have the energy available for another person's request. It's a constant weighing of priorities: no to the obvious areas that have to do with people pleasing, but yes to a woman in a coffee shop who needs more than a quick hello. No to a night meeting that puts you in a position of leaving the kids with an already-tired husband or baby-sitter, but yes to running an errand for your mother who just had knee surgery.

How can we tell the difference? It takes wisdom and discernment, and it's not always easy. One of the reasons it's so important to stay closely in touch with God's priorities and His specific call on our lives is that otherwise we have trouble knowing when to say yes and when to say no.

I think the most important thing to keep in mind when making these decisions is that God is ultimately in charge of how it all goes. It's His time, remember. He knows how we should spend our days, what our needs are, what He wants us to do. He covers our inevitable mistakes, strengthens our spirits when they sag, brings us joy as we depend on Him.

In the deepest part of my heart, I desire for my time to be spent on God's agenda: people. I don't want to be foolish, squandering the time He has given me to manage. My prayer is that I will grow so close to Christ that I can see everything with His eyes, including my schedule. And while I know I still need to manage to get the laundry done, my prayer is to say yes with a certainty that the practical does not clash with the providential. I want to say no when He needs me to and yes when that suits His purposes, and to live out my life with the open-hearted understanding that what God wills He will also make possible.

If I can start with a yes, with an attitude of "Here am I," I can trust God to do the rest.

## Time Out

• Try to think of a time during the past month or so when you have consciously given God a yes to His purpose in your life. Can you think of a time when you have passed up a God-sent appointment?

• Imagine how you will be remembered when you die. Journal some answers to these thoughts: "My husband will miss me most because . . ." "My children will always remember that I . . ." "My parents will miss the way I . . ." "My close friends will remember that I . . ."

• If this exercise was painful because you realize that people have not been a priority in your life, what can you do today to change that?

• Reread the C. S. Lewis quote. Who is your "weight of glory"? List those people in your life.

• Describe a time when responding to the needs of a person or people energized you instead of depleting you. If you didn't experience this, what do you think was wrong?

• Practically speaking, what are the ways you can distinguish between other people's priorities (which call for a no) and God's appointments (which call for a yes)?

# 22

# A Sabbath Habit:

## Building Rest and Balance into Your Family's Life

**Every summer my family** takes two short vacations. The destinations are the same every single year. Early in the summer we travel to Estes Park, Colorado, and late in the summer we travel to Leakey, Texas.

When we're in Colorado, we stay in a family cabin, which my father-in-law bought in 1983 and refurbished, adding rooms and modern plumbing. It's a hundred-year-old building full of history—Teddy Roosevelt is even rumored to have stayed there. But for all its grandiose history, it is a modest and happy place to vacation. When we're there, we hike, sit reading on the front porch (which overlooks the Rocky Mountain National Park), take in a spectacular assortment of natural wildlife, and settle into the gorgeous solitude.

Our second vacation spot is closer to home and involves my side of the family. Every Christmas my father gives our family (and my sister's and brother's families) a weeklong summer stay at River Haven Cabins on the Frio River. This summer reunion is a boisterous yet simple event. We float down the river in inner tubes, play cards, eat massive family dinners, and laugh a lot.

Everyone in the family loves our two annual summer vacations. But they're not so fond of my yearly "I'm leaving town" freak-outs. Twice every summer, about three days before we leave for vacation, I embark on the "get ready to leave town" drama. The dogs have to be carted to the vet for boarding, and the rabbit and the bird have to be taken to neighbor's homes, where they will be cared for. The mail must be stopped, the newspaper put on hold, the suitcases packed, the flowers watered, instructors notified that the kids won't be at sports lessons, loose ends tied up at work. The list goes on and on. It's no wonder that the week before we leave, I doubt we'll be going at all.

But each year I finally manage to get it all done, working feverishly to the end and holding on to anticipation of what is to come: *vacation*. There is something refreshing about seeing a new environment, breathing fresh air, and being away from regular responsibilities. Even though a lot of extra work precedes the big getaway, being able to put my feet up for a while and forget the everydayness of my home chores makes it all seem worthwhile. It's a vacation state of mind. There is a newness that my brain and my emotions and my physical body just drink in when I am on vacation.

Those vacations resemble in small ways what our family Sabbath has become to me. That weekly routine gives me the opportunity to refuel by changing the *things* I do and the way I *view* things.

But I'm getting ahead of myself. Let me tell you a little more about how our family Sabbath came about.

About five years ago, after reading and rereading the biblical references to Sabbath rest, we made a family decision to obey God by keeping the Sabbath in our own lives. I kept a journal of that experience, starting in March 2000. It was a bit of an experiment at first. We wanted to honor God in a practical way by "keeping" the Sabbath, but we were a bit confused about how to accomplish that. So there were lots of mini-experiments—like no TV. (The kids hated that one.) For a while I resisted wearing a watch to church so as not to measure time, especially during the sermon. Then there was the switch from Sunday to Saturday Sabbath to benefit my husband—after all, since he's the senior pastor of our church, Sunday is hardly a day of rest for him. At one point I worked hard to keep myself from doing laundry on our Sabbath—not because I wanted to be legalistic but because I recognized I have a laundry compulsion. I was continually loading and folding, and I wondered what I was modeling for my kids by refusing to give it a rest.

# A Sabbath Habit:
## Building Rest and Balance into Your Family's Life

We did make a point, from the very beginning, to try to make our Sabbath a positive experience—a time to enjoy pursuits that refreshed us and took us away from the daily grind. Sometimes we puttered in our garden. The kids had some creative fun videotaping made-up stories. We made a point to eat meals together as a family, and I especially enjoyed cooking new meals and soliciting help from the kids. Often we would invite friends or family over to eat with us. And we would always make a point either to read the Bible together or to talk about what God was doing in our lives.

All of this constituted the Sabbath experience at the Davises'. The purpose was to get in line with the plan God has for us. We wanted to obey Him in all things as His truth was revealed in our lives. As parents we wanted to make sure that our children understood that God's law, especially the Ten Commandments, is still vital today. At the same time, we wanted to follow Jesus' guidelines that the Sabbath was made for man and was not intended to cramp our lives with narrow legalism. That's why we felt free to move the day of our Sabbath and to try various activities that some might interpret as work.

**For several years now I have set aside every Wednesday as a Sabbath day. (My Sundays are so full of church activities and teaching that it's difficult to experience them as restful.) It took me approximately three years to accomplish the task of freeing up this day—convincing friends, associates, and myself that I really would not be doing business as usual on Wednesday. But once my "Sabbath" become established, I have seen a huge difference in my life. I don't answer the phone or go to meetings on Wednesdays. I don't schedule appointments. In fact, I don't have an agenda of any sort other than rest. I usually sleep later. I dip into the books on my nightstand. I take walks or sit in the garden and pray as God leads me. This scheduled stillness has brought a silence to my soul that has helped me understand many things that I did**

**not formerly understand. My friends have even commented on the change in me, pointing out that I have become more patient, more gentle, more thoughtful. (Donna Otto)**

Sabbath-keeping was and still is a journey for us as a family and as individual believers. If this sounds interesting and you'd like to give it a try, there are some practical things to remember before embarking on a Sabbath journey.

Just as getting ready to go on vacation takes some planning, you should prayerfully plan out how to go about changing your family's weekly schedule. If you are married, be sure to involve your husband if at all possible. If your children are old enough to understand the commandments, bring them in on discussions about what God is asking by observing a Sabbath. Study the idea of the Sabbath together before launching in on practicing it. A few tips helped me when we began some years ago.

First, understand that getting ready for the Sabbath each week can be a little like my earlier description of getting ready to go out of town, though hopefully not quite so dramatic. Usually some extra planning, extra work, some bustling about are involved in *getting ready for rest*. And if you are a wife and mother, the bulk of preparation will likely land on you. Certainly you should delegate some of the responsibilities if you can. But I think you'll find, as I have, that the reward of the Sabbath is worth the cost of preparation. You may find you need the break more than anyone else!

Second, just *abstaining* from activity is not what God calls rest. In Matthew 12:7 Jesus tells the Pharisees, "If you had known what this means, 'I desire mercy and not sacrifice,' you would have not condemned the guiltless. For the Son of Man is Lord of the Sabbath." In this verse He is quoting Hosea 6:6, in which God laments that His people are far from Him: "For I desire steadfast love and not sacrifice, the knowledge of God rather than burnt offerings."

Statements like this, I believe, free us from rigid rules for Sabbath-keeping. They remind us that God wants *us*, not some ritualistic form. He clearly states that His desire is our *steadfast love and our acknowledgment of Him*. That should be the key factor in observing the Sabbath. Every moment, every choice should be about the question, am I loving God in this or knowing more about Him? The Sabbath is not to be about abstinence; it is to be about adoration of God and re-creation for you and your family.

Third, whatever Sabbath practices you decide on, take the time to evaluate the results in your life. Psalm 119:93 says, "I will never forget your commands, for you have used them to restore my joy and health" (NLT). That is one of the chief aims of the Sabbath rest—to restore you, bring you joy, and improve your physical, mental, emotional, relational, and spiritual health. If you don't see that evidence in your life, consider changing the way you observe the Sabbath.

Fourth, over time you should begin to see a special blessing associated with your God rest. My Sabbath journals indicate that was certainly true in our family. One of my children prayed to receive Christ during one of our quiet Sundays. I referenced that we had an especially acute sense of spiritual understanding by practicing the Sabbath. That was a real blessing. I wrote in my Sabbath journal, "So many things could be done with this time, but only one is important—to obey with rest and love for God. All the stuff in my mind that keeps my body pulsating with productivity will be there tomorrow. But this—for now—is the highest form of productivity for this family."

I also was reminded that I need not strive spiritually for holiness. Exodus 31:13 says, "It helps you to remember that I am the LORD, who makes you holy" (NLT). That promise brings a sense of repose to my soul. It is not my job to produce holiness; it is only my job to follow through with God's requests.

**The Sabbath says, Stop. Look. Listen. Life is passing you by. The harder you run the more behind you get; the fuller you try to be, the more empty you become. Stop. Look. Listen. Celebrate the Sabbath. Know that you live by grace, not by work. Know that you are free. You are not a slave to necessity. Know that there is hope, that your life is moving to a grand consummation, and that it will get there by God's doing, not your own. Stop. Look. Listen. (Ben Patterson)**

Fifth, realize ahead of time that people might think you are a little odd if you change your regular life pattern. One of my friends, when apprised of our new Sabbath practice, asked half seriously, "Are you trying to become Jewish?" I laughed, but I also felt a little uncomfortable in her scrutiny. The truth is that the Sabbath is something of a lost art form, one not supported by society in general. So when you start changing your routine, people might take notice or even make comments.

Just remember that this new piece of your life is one that God asks of all Christ's followers. You are neither the first nor the last to honor God in a society that shuns Him. Just look at the book of Daniel in the Old Testament. His retort to questions about not worshiping the god of that day was to steadfastly refuse to bow to idols. In a sense you are doing just that by giving your week a day of rest—you are refusing to worship the gods of this age, the gods of calendars and commerce. If people ask, simply say that you are trying to get better balance in your family life by following what God said was His idea for optimum health and joy.

Finally, remember that Sabbath observance is *not legalism*. It is prescribed for individuals so there can be *life*. Anything that smacks of legalism should be utterly avoided. Jesus called us to mercy, not sacrifice. If you are mandating a certain form of Sabbath practice based on your understanding, it can easily become a snare of death. This is particularly true for the children in your home. Allow for a transition. And allow for some revisions. What we as a family practice now is different than the form we adhered to five years ago. One of the pieces I have let go of is that my form of rest should be every family member's best form of rest. While observing Sabbath as a family is important, so is allowing children (especially older teens) to make their own choices with spiritual guidelines. You can enforce outward compliance, but that does not necessarily produce an obedient, soft heart for God. Be very watchful of being entrapped by rules, especially if they are your own.

As an appetizer to create a longing for more, consider the words of Abraham Joshua Heschel in *The Sabbath*:

## A Sabbath Habit:
## Building Rest and Balance into Your Family's Life

Six days a week we wrestle with the world, wringing profit from the earth; on the Sabbath we especially care for the seed of eternity planted in the soul. The world has our hands, but our soul belongs to Someone Else.[1]

I love the thought of caring for the seed of eternity planted in the soul. We didn't plant it, and we cannot make it grow—God does that. But we can position ourselves to have healthy soil for the seed. Observing the Sabbath in our lives is a way of nourishing the soil. And when we do that, who knows what wonderful things might grow?

## Time Out

• Why is getting ready for rest a great way to find rest, even if the preparations are stressful?

• Why is rest not merely a matter of abstaining from certain behaviors?

• List at least three benefits your family reaps when you rest.

• Write out a statement summarizing God's objective in asking you to rest.

• How is Exodus 31:13 a verse of remembrance?

• Consider the following verses about loving God's law and about the Sabbath specifically. Read them with your family as a way of preparing to observe the Sabbath together:

—Genesis 2:1-3

—Psalm 119:1-8

—Exodus 20:8-11; 31:12-18; 34:21

—Deuteronomy 5:12-15

—Isaiah 56:6-7; 58:13-14

—Matthew 11:28-30; 12:1-14

—Mark 2:27-28

—Luke 14:1-6

—John 5:1-18; 7:14-24

# Afterword

**Well, I did it.** I managed to get my firstborn off to college.

I spent months wondering what the day would look like, how I would feel, and how Will III would fare at school. I spent months sporadically mourning what I thought would be a terminal good-bye. I tucked away all kinds of advice about specifically where to tell him good-bye at college and how to make the good-bye easier for both of us.

Then it finally happened very quickly at, of all places, an on-campus Chili's restaurant over a busy lunch hour.

My husband looked at me squarely and said, "Well, I guess you had better say good-bye."

Startled, I choked out, "Now?"

"Yes, now is a good time," he replied.

I glanced around frantically, hoping for a little more quiet, but my son looked down at me, ready for a final hug. As I reached up to embrace him, I muffled a deep sob and threw my arms around his neck. And then, deep inside, I felt this terrifying tremor as if I couldn't let go—wouldn't let go—and I burst into tears. Surprised by my sudden sobbing, my son pulled back, looked at me, and said as gently as ever, "Mom, are you OK?"

With tears now pouring down my face, I quickly looked up at him and put both of my hands on his face. "Go," I said. "And have fun. I love you so much." He started to speak, his face clouding with concern. I smiled as best I could and repeated, "Go, *please go*, and have fun." I knew that I was teetering on the edge of pure mother hysteria, desperate to keep my baby boy.

When I look back on the experience, I wish I could have had more composure. I wish I could have chosen a more suitable setting. I wish I hadn't caused my son's face to cloud up in concern. But I honestly did the best I could. And I realize that now.

I have never been in this place before, the mother of a college-aged son. I don't always know exactly what to do. But the great truth I have realized is this: I have time.

I have time because God has given me more time to be in a relationship with my son. There was no terminal good-bye, and there will be another chance to see him on campus and to be the cheerful, fun mother I would like to be. There is still time for this journey.

Upon reading this book, you too may have realized that you haven't always done everything right. Perhaps you've tried and failed to get your schedule in order. Perhaps you haven't spent your time loving God and the people in your life the way you'd like. Perhaps some events in your life have taken you by surprise and you have ended up with regrets.

I want to encourage you because, right now, you have time. You have time to get it right, to do it better. You have time to take a deep breath, whisper a prayer, and pull in closer to God as you continue on the journey toward becoming more of the person you want to be. More of the person Christ desires you to be.

Margery Williams wrote, "It doesn't happen all at once. . . .You become. It takes a long time."

How true. How I would love to read my Bible, say my prayers, and always be a "good Christian." I wish I could always please God by offering the right response and doing the right thing. And I desperately desire that I could live a life of time well spent by God's standards, offering back to Him this very gift He desires most of me.

But I'm not there yet. I'm in the process of becoming. And for me, it seems it takes a long time.

How wonderful to remember that God is well aware of our condition, that He is patiently interested in our continued growth toward Him. Perhaps that's the reason He gave us time in the first place, to give us finite mortals a framework for growing toward Him. Whatever His reasons, I know that my grateful awareness is a necessary piece of my wellness on this journey—this journey to know and love Him better.

## Afterword

"I will sing to the LORD as long as I live," sang the psalmist. "I will sing praise to my God while I have being" (Psalm 104:33).

May that be my thankful response—and yours—to the Creator of time. The God who holds our lives in His loving hands. The One who, despite our frantic failures and weary shortcomings, keeps drawing us to His patient heart.

While we have being, as we are becoming, while we have time, let us praise the Lord!

# Notes

## Chapter Two

1.  Quoted by Ellen Goodman, "Our Time-Crunch Disorder," op-ed piece posted on the *Boston Globe* web site March 27, 2005; http://www.boston.com/news/globe/editorial_opinion/oped/articles/2005/05/27/our_time_crunch_disorder. Accessed July 16, 2005.
2.  C. S. Lewis, *The Weight of Glory: And Other Addresses* (San Francisco: HarperCollins, 2001, first published 1946), 190.

## Chapter Three

1.  Anjula Razdan, "Take Your Time," *Utne*, January/February 2005, 59.

## Chapter Five

1.  Ken Gire, *Windows of the Soul* (Grand Rapids, MI: Zondervan, 1996), 19.
2.  C. S. Lewis, "Giving All to Christ," in Richard Foster and James Bryan Smith, *Devotional Classics: Selected Readings for Individuals and Groups* (San Francisco: HarperSanFrancisco, 1993), 9.

## Chapter Six

1.  Benjamin Franklin, "Daylight Saving: Letter to the Editor of the *Journal of Paris*, 1784," on daylight saving time; http://webexhibits.org/daylightsaving/franklin.html. Accessed August 8, 2005. Information about Franklin's essay was adapted for the WebExhibits site from Keith C. Heidorn, "The Elders Speak: An Economical Project," *Living Gently Quarterly* (1997, 2005), http://www.islandnet.com/~see/living/spring/franklin.htm. Accessed August 8, 2005.

## Part Two

1.  C. S. Lewis, *C. S. Lewis on Faith*, comp. Leslie Walmsley (Nashville: Thomas Nelson, 1998), 23.

## Chapter Eight

1.  Nels F. S. Ferré, *Strengthening the Spiritual Life* (New York: Harper & Brothers, 1951), 17.

## Chapter Nine

1.  Parker Palmer, *Let Your Life Speak* (San Francisco: Jossey-Bass, 2000), 55.
2.  Ibid.

## Chapter Eleven

1.  Ellen Goodman, "Time-Crunch Disorder," http://www.boston.com/news/globe/editorial_opinion/oped/articles/2005/03/27/our_time_crunch_disorder/. Accessed July 16, 2005.

## Part Three

1.  Helen Keller, *Let Us Have Faith* (Garden City, NY: Doubleday, 1950), 39.

## Chapter Thirteen

1.  John Maxwell, *Today Matters* (New York: Warner Faith, 2004), 67.
2.  Elisabeth Elliot, *Discipline: The Glad Surrender* (Old Tappan, NJ: Revell, 1982), 103.

## Chapter Fourteen

1.  Oswald Chambers, *My Utmost for His Highest* (Uhrichsville, OH: Barbour, 1992), June 9.

## Chapter Fifteen

1.  "The Afflictions of Affluence," *Newsweek* (March 20, 2004), 45.

## Chapter Twenty-one

1.  C. S. Lewis, *The Weight of Glory: And Other Addresses* (San Francisco: HarperCollins, 2001, first published 1946), 46.

## Chapter Twenty-two

1.  Abraham Joshua Heschel, *The Sabbath* (New York: Farrar, Straus and Giroux, 1979), 13.